Learning from Loss

A
Trauma-
Informed
Approach
To
Supporting
Grieving
Students

Brittany R. Collins

Heinemann
Portsmouth, NH

Heinemann

145 Maplewood Avenue, Suite 300
Portsmouth, NH 03801

www.heinemann.com

Offices and agents throughout the world

The author and publisher wish to thank those who have generously given permission to reprint
borrowed material:

Page xii: Excerpt from *A Coney Island of the Mind* by Lawrence Ferlinghetti. Copyright © 1955
by Lawrence Ferlinghetti. Reprinted by permission of New Directions Publishing Corp.

Page 79: Excerpt from "Grief Triggers" by the Coalition to Support Grieving Students. Copyright
© 2020 by the National Center for School Crisis and Bereavement. Accessed May 2020. https://
grievingstudents.org/wp-content/uploads/2020/05/NYL-4D-GriefTriggers.pdf. Reprinted by
permission of the author.

Pages 93–95: Excerpt from "Responding to Students' Personal Narratives" by Brittany R. Collins.
Originally published February 7, 2019 by Edutopia on their website. Reprinted by permission of
the George Lucas Educational Foundation.

Library of Congress Cataloging-in-Publication Data
Name: Collins, Brittany R., author.
Title: Learning from loss : a trauma-informed approach to supporting
    grieving students / Brittany R. Collins.
Description: Portsmouth, NH : Heinemann Publishing, [2021] | Includes
    bibliographical references.
Identifiers: LCCN 2021030766 | ISBN 9780325134208
Subjects: LCSH: Students—Mental health. | Students—Mental health
    services. | Bereavement in children. | Loss (Psychology) in children.
    | Grief in children. | Children—Counseling of. | Teachers—Mental health.
    | Teacher-student relationships. | School mental health services.
Classification: LCC LB3430 .C65 2021 | DDC 371.7/13—dc23
LC record available at https://lccn.loc.gov/2021030766

Editor: Louisa Irele
Production Editor: Sean Moreau
Cover and Interior Designer: Vita Lane
Typesetter: Valerie Levy, Drawing Board Studios
Manufacturing: Val Cooper

Printed in the United States of America on acid-free paper
1 2 3 4 5 CGB 25 24 23 22 21

September 2021 Printing

For Dad, in memory, and Mom, in honor.

And for Stan Samuelson, who would have
met this book with a happy dance and high
five and whose presence is deeply missed
—by me and students everywhere.

Contents

Acknowledgments

Look how far we've come.

—CHARLIE MACKESY, *THE BOY, THE MOLE, THE FOX AND THE HORSE*

Gratitude is my favorite thing. In many ways, this text is one long thank-you note—to the educators, mentors, family, and friends who have helped me learn from loss; the teachers and young people who entrusted me with their stories; and the readers whom I have yet to meet. My work is a collective effort, a product of the many communities I have been privileged to learn with and from and to whom I hope this resource offers support and salve.

Though words will never be enough, I say thank you to the following people:

- Rosetta Marantz Cohen, my Maxwell Perkins, who sat me down at her wooden table and inspired me to dream what seemed to me impossible dreams but to her, inevitabilities—this book one of them. Thank you for humor, advocacy, insight, and unceasing support. You make John Dewey proud.

- Carol Berner, for incredible wisdom and the example of what it means to educate with poise, presence, and patience. You have made a difference in my life, and for that I hold such respect, such gratitude.

- Dean Flower, who saw a writer in me ("You're not rare, but you're good."). I carry your early encouragement in my heart along with your openness to exploring loss in literature and in life. And thanks to Rick Millington, whose enthusiasm for Dickinson and Coltrane, but most of all teaching, lit a fire that sparked and sustained this book.

- Ann Van, for exemplifying what it means to embrace mystery and hold hope and for reciprocity, friendship, and insightful support (not to mention a keen review of the activities in this book). Our dads would be proud.

- Kim Evelti, for empowering me to trust my mind and heart and for the early example of leadership, professionalism, and compassion, not to mention the consistency and sincerity with which you helped me learn from loss.

- The "Zarbergs"—Abbie, Alex, and Owen (plus Willow, Xander, and RBZ)—for love, friendship, inclusion, motivation, and so much more.

- Marlee Bunch, the Frick to my Frack, for showing me how it's done! You put the best of education into practice and gave me the confidence to enter a field I'd always felt calling my name. Thank you for your enthusiasm, collaboration, and laughter along the way.

- Liz Calderone and Katri Mizula, for sisterhood, and Henry Lombino and Abel Castaño-Bravo, for sincerity and longstanding friendship.

- And the many teachers who touched my life at the Williston Northampton School and Campus School of Smith College, for sparking a life and love of learning.

   This book would not have been possible without the openness, honesty, and intellect of the teachers and practitioners who spoke with me, formally and informally—their words are woven throughout these chapters. Thank you to Priscilla Kane Hellweg; Bridget Choo; Laurel Boyd; Glenn Manning; Graham Bodie; Jeff Berman; Vicki Jay; Jana DeCristofaro; Shelly Lenn; and Velada Chaires for all that you do to empower young people. To the young writers—Kaitlyn, Payton, and Nimota—who contributed their words to these pages, thank you for sharing your artistry and insight. And to the team at Write the World, who give me a platform from which to educate, connect, and engage with teachers and students around the world, I am lucky to know and work with you.

Thank you to Louisa Irele for seeing a book in me and guiding me toward it with precision, expertise, and encouragement, and to the rest of the Heinemann team for their hard work and belief in this book. I know I speak for educators everywhere when I say that I am grateful for all that you do.

Finally, my family: to Grammy and in memory of Tom, to Grandma and in memory of Boppa, to Mom and in memory of Dad, thank you for raising me with strength, courage, and a wellspring of love.

Carpe Diem.

Introduction

Given this diagnosis, I find many people ask me how I am when actually they are asking, "How do you deal with it?" or "How hard is it?" Because cancer is such a difficult topic to discuss, and because many people have difficulty simply approaching difficult subjects, I use the catch phrase Carpe Diem as a small, impactful, motivational way for people to change their focus from the problem and associated difficulties of the disease, to something a bit more productive and positive. Carpe Diem, or Seize the Day, reminds us that tomorrow is not a guarantee, and that we should live in the present and be thankful and productive for who we are and what we are today.

—JEFF COLLINS

A Poem, a Teacher, a Parent

At the age of fifteen, as a sophomore in high school, I sat in English class on the third floor of a tall brick schoolhouse, looking through the window at a mountain range in the distance. During the class periods that fell before lunch, when my stomach was grumbling and the haze of morning sleepiness was just starting to lift, I often found myself imagining that Victor Frankenstein's monster roamed those very mountains, so similar were their clouded crags to the cover image on Mary Shelley's book, Caspar David Friedrich's romantic painting *Wanderer Above the Sea of Fog*.

One morning in spring, my soon-to-retire English teacher, Mr. Latham, passed warm photocopies of beat poet Lawrence Ferlinghetti's "The World Is a Beautiful Place" around our class-room—a piece featured in his 1958 collection *A Coney Island of the Mind*. From his wooden podium at the front of our desks, he read aloud the verse in a slow, measured tone:

> The world is a beautiful place
> to be born into
> if you don't mind some people dying
> all the time. (93)

It was a dark poem, yet witty in its solemnity, and I reveled in Ferlinghetti's attention to the particular. I smiled at the conclusion of the verse, albeit an arguably somber meditation on mortality, and Mr. Latham asked me why.

"Brittany, you smiled! What made you smile?!" he said in what seemed a tone of both shock and relief.

I could not answer his question. I merely knew that something inside of me felt seen and understood. I feigned some response about sentence structure and tone, but the real impact of the poem remained inarticulable for years.

The summer before I entered Mr. Latham's classroom, I lost my father to breast cancer while my mother endured her own chemotherapy. I was fourteen at the time of my father's death, and I spent my summer days intentionally distracted, poring over pages of *The Catcher in the Rye* while at my father's bedside. My dad was a reader. As a child, we spent rainy afternoons bonding amid the stacks at Barnes and Noble. At his bedside, there were always biographies heavy as bricks and beside them piles of his own scrawled journals—letters to me and my mom that he wrote every night after his stage IV diagnosis.

Should teachers address students' social-emotional concerns and, if so, how? To what extent? Will those concerns take time and energy away from curricular content? In an era when teachers already face a plethora of demands and challenges—standards to meet, tests to plan for, scores to compare, time limitations to work around—do topics like grief really belong on teachers' plates? Should schools seek to cordon those facets of students' experiences in the offices of school psychologists and external therapists? Should the social-emotional and intellectual cohere in the classroom—and, if so, how much?

These questions grew out of my experiences sitting in Mr. Latham's classroom, reading Ferlinghetti. Or perhaps they grew out of an experience I had months earlier, when I told my father that I loved him and set a bookmark amid Mr. Antolini's words in Salinger's text. Or maybe they started to simmer because I remember how it felt to be a sixth grader whose father had just been diagnosed with an anomalous disease that teachers wanted to talk about and friends (and I) did not. I'm not sure.

I do know, however, that my experiences as a student sparked a lifelong fascination with identity development, the ways in which the stories of lives both fictional and real shape and define our reality, provide catharsis, or provoke conversation. They drove my interests in social-emotional learning and interdisciplinary writing curricula, which led me into my first undergraduate education program out of high school. They brought me home to my dad, into the pages of the stories that he read and wrote. And they set pen to paper, inspiring me to scratch out some stories of my own.

When I sat in Mr. Latham's class on that foggy spring morning, pink backpack by my feet, I could not know that the reading of one poem would steer my path beyond those walls. As I folded my photocopied poem hamburger style and tucked it into my three-ring binder, the metal rings snapping shut their teeth, I could not know that I carried a center point of my future scholarship, my future career.

Today, I look back at Ferlinghetti's words and hear Mr. Latham's in my mind—urging me to explain my reaction, to delve into the effect and affect of language. I remember him nudging me to take Advanced Placement English in the coming years and how meaningful it was that someone believed in my abilities. I sit humbled by the power of a poem, the power of a teacher, and the power of a parent to inform and transform the life of a young learner. And I sit with the truth that the thread of mortality that was woven throughout my language arts education was, for me, not an inappropriately morose focus of my adolescent learning, as critics of "death education" may suggest, but rather an invitation to explore and make meaning of that which comprises a life well lived.

Love and loss are two sides of a quarter—oppositional, yet inseparable—and they strike at the core of what it means to be alive. I am able to recognize the coexistence of tragedy and meaning because teachers and authors lifted those topics up to the light, in their own ways, throughout my time in school. They reified Walt Whitman's (1891) quote, "That the powerful play goes on, and you may contribute a verse," written in *Leaves of Grass* and later popularized through the teachings of fictional English teacher Mr. Keating in *Dead Poets Society*.

Learning from Loss is my verse.

In the United States, seven out of ten teachers have a student in their classroom who is grieving (Nadworny 2015), and loss is the most frequently reported category of trauma experienced by young people (Pynoos et al. 2014, 11–12). It is unlikely that any educator, whether a preservice elementary teacher or a tenured college professor, will complete an academic year—let alone a career—without the heavy coat of loss making its way into the classroom, on the back of a student if not on their own shoulders. I suspect you're picking up this book because you are one such educator, teaching one or more students who are muddling through the throes of grief as I was at fourteen. For you, the reality of loss is all too real; perhaps you are sad, scared, unsure of where to begin.

This book is here for you. As you approach and engage with this text, I hope that you come to treat it as your space—a safe space—within which to grapple, question, breathe, and prepare for the challenges and rewards of supporting grieving students in times of need. I know firsthand the longitudinal power and potential of an educator's empathic efforts; it is because of such efforts that I am writing this book today. Yet so, too, do I appreciate the seeming impossibility of tackling the topic of grief with students, and welcome ambivalence as a reaction to this work. It is these three entities—power, potential, and (im)possibility—that we will explore together in the pages that follow.

At first glance, this may seem to be a book about death. But I contend that it is equally a book about life—and the light of it. So often, times of sorrow bring into sharp focus what we value most in this world: connection, laughter, learning—all of which comprise classroom life. When grief disrupts this energy, in whatever form, we ache. Simultaneously, the most valuable tenets of our lives—the delight, the meaning—become richer and more necessary.

I believe that together we have the power to persist through the challenges posed by the presence of grief in schools and to do so mindfully, with compassion, while supporting our own needs, too. We owe this to ourselves as well as our students—for school may be all they have.

The following chapters will guide you through the balance that is the what, why, and how of grief support in a schooling context, from the logistical to the interpersonal and curricular. You will engage in writing exercises geared toward self-exploration and social-emotional awareness to better understand how loss impacts your teaching. We will look at lesson plans, activities, and teaching strategies for creating grief-responsive classrooms and pedagogies across grade levels, from action protocols for the days after a loss occurs; conversational strategies with which to approach parents, guardians, students, and colleagues; resources for cultivating resiliency and social-emotional well-being in all students, including those who are grieving; to wellness strategies that seek to protect and replenish teachers' hearts. This volume—grounded in extensive reading, research, interviews, as well as my own experience—will provide you with the tools you need to approach the tender work of teaching about and around loss, no matter its form.

Before we begin, it is relevant to inquire about the teacher's role regarding grief in the school system. In 1999, two armed teenagers opened fire at a high school in Littleton, Colorado, committing the deadliest high school shooting in history up to that point (History.com editors 2009). In the era that has since ensued, we have seen more than 141 children, educators, and staff members killed; 287 injured; and 215,000 students at 217 schools "subject[ed] to active shooter violence" (Coleman 2018, 6). On September 11, 2001, parents, teachers, nurses, and guidance counselors walked into classrooms with the impossible task of telling students that an act of terror had occurred in New York. Life was irreparably altered—a void rang loud.

I wrote most of this book nineteen years later, in 2020, amid a global pandemic and racial justice movement that continue to impact not only the ways we teach, learn, and build supportive relationships with young people but also force us all to reckon with loss in new and piercing ways. It is a dire but crucial fact that loss is not only an entity that students and teachers carry with them into school but now, also, an entity that can and does occur *at* school. By virus or violence, the past year alone has changed our communities and caused us to pause.

A study conducted by the American Federation of Teachers and New York Life Foundation in July and August 2020, for example, revealed that 26 percent of surveyed teachers had already lost someone in their school community to COVID-19. Ninety-three percent expected the pandemic would have long-term traumatic impacts on students—an instinct confirmed by leading trauma researcher Bessel van der Kolk, who shared on New Hampshire Public Radio that the isolation and perceived immobility incited by the pandemic created "'pre-trau-matic conditions' in the brain" (McOwen 2020). Ninety-five percent of teachers said that they—like you—would like to do more to support their grieving students. Yet only 15 percent felt prepared to do so (AFT and New York Life Foundation 2020).

This discomfort is understandable. The topic of grief support remains absent in most teacher preparation programs, with fewer than 1 percent of teachers reporting grief-related training in their undergraduate or graduate education courses (AFT and New York Life Foundation 2012, 4). Amid the demands of standards, test scores, performance reports, and the countless other commitments that tug on teachers' time, it can feel daunting to address the topic of loss in schools. But teachers realize that the issue of managing grief in the classroom seems no longer a question of *if* or *should* but *when* and *how*: How can teachers best scaffold the topic and experience of loss to support young learners in the face of fear and sadness? When a student loses a parent, or a faculty loses a colleague, or a school shooting occurs too close to home, what should we do? What should we say? How can classroom teachers and administrators collaborate most effectively with trained psychologists, counselors, or crisis response teams so that a school's support efforts are successful?

Teachers need opportunities to commune, collaborate, and communicate about the challenges and rewards of encountering and addressing loss with their students if we are ever to work toward the creation of schools in which grieving students feel safe, welcomed, and respected. Your selecting this book makes me think that I am in like-minded company and that your seeking out resources on this topic means you already have the tools you need—the sincerity, the motivation—to succeed in supporting grieving students no matter any hesitations you may feel.

To ground our time together, I've written some guiding beliefs and intentions that center me as I approach grief work. As the teaching and learning coordinator at Write the World, an online writing education platform, I engage middle and high school students and teachers in synchronous and asynchronous educational programming. Though I do not teach students in a traditional classroom or work as a psychologist, I bring to this text an awareness of the ways in which teaching transcends the classroom: Whether you are a coach, advisor, dorm parent, online educator, curriculum writer, school bus driver, teacher, or administrator, your work is valid. Your support of grieving students is necessary. And you have the power to make a difference in the lives of young people. Your role will be different from that of a school counselor or psychologist but no less important; I use the proverbial "we" in these pages to encompass the many roles education professionals take, all of them relevant in the discussion we are about to have.

I invite you to dip into this practice by creating bulleted lists of your own—which may add onto or look quite different from those that follow. Return to them throughout your reading and teaching experiences for a reminder—especially in the face of a critical decision—of your *why* in relation to this work.

GUIDING BELIEFS

- Grief work is essential in a classroom context; we have a responsibility to pay attention to the presence and impact of loss in our learning environments.

- Grief is not a problem to be fixed or avoided, but a reality to embrace and approach.

- Teachers and students engaging in grief work deserve to feel validated and valued.

- Teachers and students engaging in grief work need room to make and repair mistakes.

- Grief-responsive classroom practices benefit all students, regardless of whether they're enduring a loss.

- Grief is a challenging topic. It's natural for students and teachers to feel nervous.

- Avoidance is a natural coping mechanism that often perpetuates pain.

- When we lose the ones we love, they're not wholly gone; their gifts are siphoned through us, out into the world.

INTENTIONS

- I intend to approach grief work openly and honestly.

- I intend to welcome all experiences and perspectives, especially those that contradict or challenge my own.

- I intend to ask not "How did I do?" but "What can I learn from this?"*

- I intend to extend my comfort zone through sharing experiences.

- I intend to honor my own and others' limits.

---

*In college, a mentor and teacher extraordinaire shared this piece of wisdom as I prepared for a challenging presentation. It's since guided my approach to teaching and learning and to life.

Pause and Ponder

What are your guiding beliefs when you consider the topic of grief in the classroom? Based on your own loss experiences and those of your students, what truths do you hold? What intentions do you hope to set as you reflect upon and look toward opportunities to work with students who are grieving? Make your own bulleted lists. Return to these points as guiding pillars throughout this book or when grief work in your classroom feels tenuous or overwhelming.

Grief Work: A Gordian Knot**

Though much of American education is standardized, there is no prescriptive way to support grieving students in any classroom or learning community. It would be reductive to condense the nuance and granularity of grief to step-by-step strategies or social-emotional edicts, given its contextual and interpersonal variations. But this should not preclude our exploring or promote our ignoring general principles and strategies that can support our approaches to grief work. Research shows, for example, that all children need safe places and people with whom to investigate these topics, and school is one such constant amid chaos where young people may find safety. "Limiting discussion about death will only hinder children's understanding of the loss and interfere with their ability to cope with it," writes David J. Schonfeld (1993, 269), pediatrician and founder of the National Center for School Crisis and Bereavement. "Children need caring and knowledgeable adults with whom they can discuss death, both in a general context before a loss and specifically in response to a significant death" (269).

**Gordian knot is a term used to describe a complex situation. Stemming from the story of Alexander the Great, it is a metaphor for seemingly unsolvable problems, or knots that only become more tangled as one tries to loosen them (Andrews 2018).

Many times, in the writing of this book, I found myself surveying research and reaching toward suggested strategies that my adolescent, grieving self would not have found helpful. I am humbled by how quickly my adult mind lets go of the intense reservations and hesitations that I felt in my core as a kid. Had you met me at ten years old, when my father was diagnosed, or at fifteen, after he passed, and attempted to initiate any kind of check-in, you would've found yourself immersed in a conversation that went something like this:

> **Caring adult:** So, how are you doing?
>
> **Me:** Good.
>
> **Caring adult:** But how are you really doing? [*Drawn-out pause.*]
>
> **Me** [*Blushing*]: Good.
>
> **Caring adult:** And how's your mom?
>
> **Me** [*Blushing, fidgeting*]: She's good.

We're really getting somewhere, aren't we?

I'm sure that all of us, if we think reflectively, can identify ways in which our relationships with loss have shifted across time and contexts. A coping strategy that may have worked once may prove unhelpful, even harmful, years later. Sometimes, we may feel best left alone, processing and persisting on our own; other times, we may crave connection. Every loss is different, and as we navigate the progression from immediate grief to eventual acceptance and adaptation (though it's important to note—and we'll explore this later—that the five stages of grief are no longer considered an accurate framework, because grief is more cyclical and continual than their confines imply), we'll find ourselves, as well as our students, undulating between emotions, coping mechanisms, and outlooks.

Because grief is such a complex process, bereaved students may send mixed signals in the classroom—moving, like centripetal and centrifugal forces, toward and away from intimate honesty and avoidant denial. When we witness such a shifting inner landscape, it can feel hard to know which tendency to cater to, especially when we may move toward and away from grief ourselves, our own comfort zones and receptivity fluctuating in patterns that may not always align with those of our students.

Having grown up a dancer, I'm reminded of a contemporary contact improv class that I took as a freshman in college, which was—let me tell you—out of my comfort zone. My classmates and I bustled into a boathouse overlooking a pond both murky and smooth, stepping barefoot out of winter boots and onto the wooden floor. A pianist sat perched in the corner, each day his tempo and tone manifesting in the moment. We created accompanying movement, responding to one another's kinesthetic choices to create story lines both subjective and cohesive. It felt intimidating, in the first weeks of class, to take up space in this way—to become comfortable with stillness, to resist filler movements and to view each pause as a tool. Integrating the contact nature of the course posed an even greater challenge, requiring me to not only reckon with my vulnerability but become open and responsive to that of others. Yet by the end of the term, my classmates and I were tackling lifts without language.

There seems some parallel between this class and the Gordian knot of grief support: neither allows for foolproof planning nor scripted participation or conversation, but both operate around a certain set of rules (or, better to say, suggestions)—a subliminal choreography that informs execution. As we shift toward the *why* and *how* of grief work in the coming pages, I encourage you to return to your intents and your beliefs as a dancer might a lunge or leap. This work requires a delicate calibration between strength and softness, intellect and emotion, movement and stillness, proximity and space. So, too, does it necessitate organic collaboration. Practice supports performance, as well as process, and it is the latter that is our goal.

Laurel Boyd, a dance teacher whom I interviewed for this book and who helped me through my own grief in high school, offered a resonant frame with which to begin our work. "I think collaboration is the essence of education," she told me, seated in an office tucked toward the back of her studio. She continued:

> It has to be that way; otherwise it just feels like an imposition, like stuff is just cut and pasted or imposed or pushed on [students].
> Sometimes we focus so much on the content that we forget about the humanity that's supposed to be absorbing it. I never wanted to lose the dancer for the dance. I never

wanted to place the work as more important than the person, the human in front of me who is also in development, also in process. . . . I can't do what I do unless there are humans who are meeting me in that field.

Write and Reflect

Take five minutes to think about someone close to you who is no longer with us—a teacher, student, parent, partner, friend. What is your favorite memory of this person? What is the most powerful lesson this person taught you? How have you passed this person's legacy on through your own work and life?

Next, consider this: What strengths do you bring to your work with grieving students? What about this work proves most challenging or daunting for you and why? What about your life and loss experiences informs these strengths and challenges?

Grief Glossary: Some Notes on Terminology

Throughout this book, I use a few key terms. You can find out more about them here.

GRIEVING VERSUS BEREAVED

I use the terms *grieving* and *bereaved* somewhat interchangeably throughout the text. Bereavement is typically used to describe someone who has lost a family member (e.g., a bereaved student might be one whose mother recently died). Grief—and grieving—apply more broadly to anyone experiencing loss, even if that loss is not tied to a death. Following are three types of non-death-related losses that you might recognize from your own life or learning environment; the teaching strategies we explore in this book are relevant for supporting students dealing with these and other types of loss, too.

Living Losses

Living losses encompass those departures, absences, or separations that create a grief response in our brains and bodies even though they do not involve the death of a person. For example, a student whose mother is serving in the military, whose sibling is incarcerated, whose parents are getting divorced, who is estranged from a relative, or who is disconnected from key caretakers because of COVID-19 may experience grief and trauma responses that are as legitimate as those experienced after the death of a loved one (Harris and Winokuer 2019, 121–37).

Secondary Losses

Secondary losses occur as collateral damage in the wake of an overarching death, tragedy, or loss, and, similar to living losses, do not always involve the absence of a person. For example, after a parent dies, a student may be forced to contend with a change in housing or schooling, a familial falling out that leaves relatives and support systems astray, or a shift in socioeconomic status that disrupts that student's home environment. These layers of loss are connected to but separate from the primary loss. They complexify the social-emotional and potentially traumatic effects of that loss and may position students for increased behavioral or cognitive challenges in the classroom (Williams 2013).

Disenfranchised Grief

The term *disenfranchised grief* describes forms of grief and loss that are not socially or societally acknowledged. One might experience disenfranchised grief over a miscarriage, a move, a breakup, a loss of health or ability, or even a loss that one is not directly connected to—for example, one that occurs within one's schooling community. Because these types of losses are societally silenced and often stigmatized, they typically involve added stress and social discomfort (Thelen 2007).

(continues)

(continued)

GRIEF WORK ──────────────────────────────

I use the term *grief work* to refer to the practice of implementing trauma-informed, grief-responsive strategies in the classroom. This term is meant to emphasize the active, evolving nature of engaging with and learning from loss in a learning community. Notably, the term *grief work* was once adapted from Freud's 1917 phrase "the work of mourning," to imply that all bereaved people endure a laborious process of working through and recovering from loss—a notion that gave way to Kübler-Ross' grief stages in the twentieth century. Modern grief science has largely disproved this notion of progressive work, realizing that grief is more fluid and evolving and that the majority of people experience healthy adaptation, therefore delegitimizing the term *grief work* in psychological and medical spheres (Bonanno 2009, 14–15).

When I use it in this book, I do not mean the Freudian notion of personal progression through grief, but instead the much simpler notion that teachers are pursuing active pedagogical work when they choose to implement grief-responsive strategies in the classroom.

TRAUMA-INFORMED VERSUS GRIEF-RESPONSIVE ──────────

I use the terms *trauma-informed* and *grief-responsive* interchangeably. This is to emphasize that not all grief is traumatic, and not all trauma involves grief, yet trauma-informed and grief-responsive pedagogies are adaptable to both populations of students. Throughout grief literature, the term *grief-sensitive* is used in relation to school districts and teaching pedagogies, but I instead offer *grief-responsive* as a term to imply more active and intentional engagement by the teacher-practitioner (i.e., we are not merely being sensitive to the presence of grief in the classroom, but are actively responding to our awareness of that grief by making the decision to shape our learning environments accordingly).

When a Student Is Grieving, What's Going On?

A Look Inside the Bereaved Brain

You never completely get over the loss. . . . It's like having a broken leg that never heals perfectly—that still hurts when the weather gets cold, but you learn to dance with the limp.

—ANNE LAMOTT, "AN HOMAGE TO AGE AND FEMININITY"

"I t was around 1998," began Priscilla Kane Hellweg, educator and executive director of Enchanted Circle Theater, a nonprofit, multi-service arts organization based in Holyoke, Massachusetts.

I was a teaching artist at the Morgan School here in the flats in Holyoke. It was the second day of an artist-in-residence program. I was in first grade, and the day before I was to arrive for the second day, I got a call from the teacher to say that there was a terrible tragedy and Jonathan had been killed. He was sleigh riding and got hit by a car.

I said, "Well, I'm happy to come in if you would like me there, and I'm happy to not come in if you would like to have the class to yourself," and her voice quivered.

She said, "I would love for you to be there. I'm really afraid of facing the class. I think I'm just going to fall apart."

So, I came in, and they all sat down on the rug, and I said, "I understand that there's been a terrible tragedy, and that your friend Jonathan has been killed in an accident. I didn't get a chance to know him." I asked them all if they would tell me things about him. "Think about your friend Jonathan. What would you like me to know?"

The first person said he was a really great soccer player, and he could hit the ball faster than anybody. Somebody else said, "He was my best friend, and he made me laugh."

Somebody else said, "He was really good at math. Anytime I needed help, I would go to Jonathan, and he would help."

We went around the circle, and everybody had something to say, and everybody was really listening. There [were] probably twenty-eight kids in the class, and [their] teacher was in the circle. She was listening, tears streaming down her face, and she said, "He was a tender soul, and I will hold him in my heart."

And then the last child said something like, "He had the best sense of humor of anybody I knew," and then she said, "So, can we play ball now?" referring to the day before, [when] I taught them a game of imaginary ball.

My takeaway was they were really interested in talking about [the loss] and sharing with me, a stranger, about their friend. But then they also didn't want to get lost in that. They

Learning from Loss

didn't want to get stuck in it. They had an experience of
sharing. There would be more sharing. There were counselors
in the room, and the nurse was there, so [the teacher] had
her supports, but I think it helped to have an outside voice.
I think it was helpful for them each to have a little bit to say.
And then that was it.

   I wasn't sure how to bridge it. You talk about a child
"passing" a lot. It felt very important to me to actually, without
a lot of my own sort of stuff around it, to be able to say, "I
understand there was a tragedy, and Jonathan died," and
they didn't bat an eyelash.

   That was important for me.

Priscilla's story offers a snapshot of the ways in which a community
of learners can grapple with grief together. Her words demonstrate
how an attentive team of caring professionals can support the
regulation and processing of young people. But what exactly happens
in those moments when a death is announced and the mind begins
to process the meanings of *before* and *after*, *here* and *not here*?
What can we learn from that first grader who asked, "So, can we
play ball now?" Was she being dismissive? Resilient? Or was her
question representative of more complex neural and developmental
processes going on beneath the surface? And what does all of this
have to do with adolescence? How can secondary school teachers
apply knowledge of neurobiology to best support students who are
experiencing grief and trauma in the teenage years?

Grief and Bereavement: The Basics

In this chapter, we'll take a look inside the grieving brain to better
understand the biological and behavioral responses the body experiences after loss. We'll consider the intersections of trauma, grief,
and toxic stress, and we'll weave our knowledge together to explore
practical applications and activities for creating classroom environments supportive of all students, including those who are grieving.
Let's begin with some background info.

Grief is a Natural Response to Many Kinds of Losses

Grief does not, in itself, constitute trauma or pathology. Humans are relational creatures: a held hand, a burst of laugher, a knowing glance—these are the things that let us know we are alive. From our earliest days, our brains are shaped by the people and environments around us (Center on the Developing Child n.d.). As we grow, we form attachments with caregivers, friends, and romantic partners; we shape and are shaped by others' behaviors; and we respond, inevitably, to stress, loss, and pain.

The bonds we forge with others not only promote or negate healthy development but are also encoded in our brains. Studies conducted using fMRI scans show that social attachments involve neural mechanisms in the reward center of the brain (Shulman 2018, 97). When we lose someone to whom we are attached, we feel that loss in part because of alterations in this wiring; we go through a kind of visceral relational withdrawal.

We may also experience grief in response to other kinds of losses and life transitions: graduating from school, moving to a new city, leaving a job. Such a response is, again, valid, natural, and often based in neurology.

Loss Changes Our Environments Which Compounds Grief

In the wake of a death, we often experience secondary losses—changes in our surroundings and routines that reflect the absence of the person we have lost. We no longer hear the sound of a parent's car pulling into the driveway after work; smell a grandmother's perfume; feel the surety of a sister checking homework before bed. There's a change in housing or school or even a familial falling out. We do not often recognize the sensory components of our relationships until they are removed, nor how these cues—sounds, sights, smells, tastes—make us feel. When a student is grieving, they are not only mourning the person who has died but adjusting to disrupted routines that lack these "hidden regulators" (Di Ciacco 2008, 25) that—in the context of positive relationships—once helped them maintain their emotional well-being, if subconsciously.

Grief Does Not Follow Five Stages

In 1969, Elisabeth Kübler-Ross introduced the five stages of grief—denial, anger, bargaining, depression, and acceptance—marking a pivotal moment in the normalization and study of grief (2014, 34); however, further research disproved her theory, revealing that the human brain oscillates between all stages of grief in a nonlinear pattern. We mourn and make meaning of our losses in bursts, especially at a young age (Bonanno 2009, 39), and these bursts allow us to move between confrontation and avoidance, grappling with the depths of loss one moment, then asking, in our own ways: "So, can we play ball now?" Our brains have evolved to self-protect in this way, immersing us incrementally in the reality of loss until we can see, to quote the poem "Kindness" by Naomi Shihab Nye, "the size of the cloth" (1995, 42).

There is no timeline for when these bursts recede, nor should we impart or imply a timeline regarding students' expressions of grief at school. Humans re-grieve on occasions of significance (the anniversary of a loved one's death, parents' day at school, holiday vacation, graduation, etc.), and young people often experience exacerbated grief during developmental milestones to which a loved one would have borne witness. Grief, then, is a lifelong process. Its intensity dulls, and the majority of us integrate loss experiences and past memories into the narratives of our lives; adapt to an altered reality; make meaning of losses and relationships through storytelling; and move forward without suffering psychological harm. But this does not mean that we emerge unchanged or even that we emerge at all. Rather, we learn to live an altered reality. To "dance with the limp." To re-story our lives.

Grief Impacts the Brain and Body

Grief activates the same brain regions as physical pain (Shulman 2018, 94) and impacts the body in two ways: a fight-or-flight response involving the endocrine, immune, and autonomic nervous

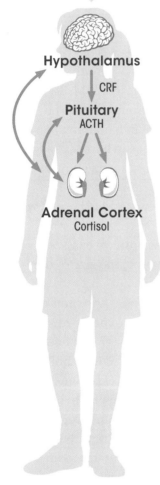

Stress Response

Hypothalamus

CRF

Pituitary
ACTH

Adrenal Cortex
Cortisol

CRF = corticotropin-releasing factor
ACTH = adrenocorticotropic hormone

Figure 1–1   The HPA Axis

systems; and a depressive response involving memory, sleep, attention, self-regulation, and executive functioning (NBC News 2018; Low 2020). It is not only emotional but physical.

We have known for a long time that the HPA axis, which connects our central nervous and endocrine systems, as pictured in Figure 1–1, is central to our stress response as well as its hormonal and immune-related implications (Tough 2012, 12; Alschuler 2016). Another part of our nervous system, the vagus nerve, which connects our brain, lungs, heart, stomach, and intestines, is thought to also play an important role in our response to stress (Wagner 2016). We physically feel grief and pain in our mind, heart, and gut, because they quite literally impact these areas of the body by way of our vagus nerve (Porges 2009, 86; van der Kolk 2014, 80).

Loss Can Have a Lifelong Impact on Teens

When teens lose people they love, the impact can pose a special threat to their development and lifelong health, especially when paired with chronic stress or adversity (Tough 2012, 13; van der Kolk 2014, 242; Burke Harris 2018, 73; Shulman 2018, 98). To better understand teens' responses to loss and trauma, it is important to know about adverse childhood experiences, or ACEs: The ACE survey, developed in 1990, is now a leading tool in scientists' efforts to understand how "environments," rather than "experiences," may preclude healthy development. One's "ACE score," essentially the number of childhood traumatic experiences one has endured, increases the risk of developing later-life illness—cancer, heart disease, diabetes, depression, and substance abuse, among other conditions (Starecheski 2015). Nearly two-thirds of adults surveyed had experienced at least one ACE, and more than one in five participants had experienced three ACEs or more (Centers for Disease Control 2020). The aftereffects of loss can linger in the body for a lifetime, especially when paired with additional or persistent trauma. We'll return to this idea—as well as explore the shortcomings of the ACE model—in chapters to come.

Grief Can Be Traumatic

Trauma is determined, not by a specific type of event or experience, but by the nervous system's response to an event or experience (Souers & Hall 2016, 15-16). The American Psychological Association defines *trauma* as "an emotional response to a terrible event" (2021); and the Substance Abuse and Mental Health Services Administration defines it as "an event, series of events, or set of circumstances that is experienced by an individual as physically or emotionally harmful or life threatening and that has lasting adverse effects on the individual's functioning and mental, physical, social, emotional, or spiritual well-being" (2019).

Our understandings of trauma are changing alongside lexical evolution. In the latest edition of the *Diagnostic and Statistical Manual of Mental Disorders*, the *DSM-5*, post-traumatic stress disorder (PTSD) has its own category (Pai, Suris, and North 2017, 7). Its clinical definitions, once subjective, now contain specific criteria psychologists can use to make diagnoses, including "exposure to actual or threatened death" (Forman-Hoffman et al. 2016).

Socially, our perceptions are changing, too. We no longer regard trauma as something reserved for those who have fought in combat. We know that quotidian routines can comprise their own battles, and it no longer seems far-fetched that grief could qualify as, or lead to, "an emotional response to a terrible event."

In other words, yes, grief can be traumatic.

But because trauma is a response to an *event*, one student may find loss traumatic while a classmate does not. Diverse responses to loss experiences are normal and not within students' control. If a student is traumatized by a loss, it does not mean that they are weaker or less resilient than their peer, but rather that a combination of factors (genetics, presence of a support system, contextual challenges and inequities, prior losses or traumas) predispose certain populations to the privilege of resolution and recalibration and others to prolonged, even chronic, grief and trauma.

Grief Changes Behavior

Students with grieving brains have different neurological landscapes than their non-grieving selves and non-grieving peers, and they may exhibit a number of behavioral changes—and challenges—in the classroom (see Figure 1–2). Because of the fight-flight-or-freeze response, students will have a much harder time with higher-

Emotional and Behavioral Responses to Grief or Trauma

anger

avoidance

guilt

anxiety

fear

sadness

numbness

denial

attention seeking

connection seeking

impaired sense of future

physical health complaints (headaches, nausea)

helplessness

hopelessness

desire for control (can manifest in myriad ways; some, such as perfectionism, might be reinforced within an academic context)

self-destructive behaviors

apathy

catastrophizing

people pleasing

(Adapted from Ehmke n.d.; Fernández-Alcántara et al. 2016, 1; NASP School Safety and Crisis Response Committee 2015; Jacobs n.d.)

Figure 1–2 Responses to Grief and Trauma

functioning processes like thinking, reasoning, managing emotions, and reining in their impulses. Similar to students experiencing trauma, they might feel an impaired sense of physical and emotional safety; a loss or lack of connection and trust in their relationships; and an impaired ability to manage or regulate their emotions (Shear 2012, 119–28; Shulman 2018; Di Ciacco 2008).

Teaching Strategies to Enact Right Away

With time and consistency, teachers can support grieving students as they make their way back to higher functioning. Schools have the opportunity to intervene in loss processes by creating spaces that are supportive of students' adaptation and offer stability amid a new and swirling world. The pedagogical practices presented throughout this book promote the well-being of all learners, regardless of whether they have a history of loss or trauma, validating the implementation of trauma-informed, grief-responsive approaches on a broad scale. Here are some strategies that are readily implementable in classrooms; we will explore more in chapters to come.

Apply an Asset-Based Lens to Challenging Behaviors

Rather than punish or judge the behaviors depicted in Figure 1–2, recognize that they are adaptive coping mechanisms meant to serve a purpose: dulling pain, fulfilling an unmet need, reclaiming control in the face of instability. Maxwell's temper might serve him well when he is protecting his cousin from an abusive partner, just as Miranda's attention seeking might eke out the focus of her recently widowed mother who works two jobs to keep their family together in a one-bedroom apartment. We have all lived through hard things, and in the face of hard things, we do our best. Teens, too, are doing their best. We can help them by creating supportive environments, teaching and modeling healthy coping mechanisms, and respecting their own efforts to seek salve and survival. Challenging behaviors are almost always creative solutions; they just become maladaptive outside of the contexts for which they were developed.

Consider Context

Although we will investigate strategies that fall within the realm of trauma-informed, grief-responsive teaching, we must not over-simplify or turn away from the complexity, nuance, and pervasiveness of those factors that lead to grief and trauma in the first place. "We are in a tremendously tumultuous time in education," shared Priscilla. She continued:

> In every single classroom we go to, there is trauma. It's not just urban—it is urban, rural, suburban. Sometimes it is pervasive. Sometimes trauma is event-based, and sometimes it is environment-based. The ongoing level of trauma really impacts the way students learn.

The ACE study revealed that regardless of racial identity, socioeconomic standing, or gender, childhood trauma poses a serious threat to the entire US population, but some people are more prone to toxic stress because of structural inequities that may also beget loss—racism, racial violence, and poverty posing just a few examples (Burke Harris 2018, 193).

When the context of bereavement intersects with further trauma, one's ACE score skyrockets. If a student's mother dies as a result of domestic violence, their ACE score will rise. If that student is also a victim of verbal or physical abuse, their number will continue to ascend. In communities where violence is rife, traumatic losses can occur on a daily basis, flicking students' fight-flight-or-freeze response on and into survival mode for indefinite amounts of time. For many, survival mode is not a euphemism: in the United States alone, an estimated three million children witness gun violence every year, and over eighteen thousand children are shot, experiencing injury or death (Everytown Research and Policy 2019). We cannot underestimate the prevalence, nor the gravity, of this crisis. And we cannot excuse ourselves from the work of fighting for a solution.

While public awareness of trauma's ubiquity grows, there is also increasing recognition that the ACE survey, though helpful, has its limitations. Chronic stress that does not check the ACE score boxes, like "racism, homophobia or other systemic injustices," can still dampen the immune system or impact mental well-being beyond childhood, leading to the behavioral challenges and later-life health issues that we previously explored (Gaffney 2019). Skepticism surrounding the oversimplification of trauma is not limited to ACE metrics but extends to interventional teaching strategies born out of them, like character development centered on "grit," which we will explore in chapters to come. For our purposes, ACEs offer a starting point; we realize that they are not comprehensive but represent some of the circumstances that lead to students' losses, that manifest as behavioral challenges in our classrooms and caring relationships, and that require our consideration when working to reach bereaved students at school. We recognize that adversities not included in ACE metrics are equally urgent and valid, and that their health implications are profound. And we are mindful that students who come from circumstances that induce chronic stress before or after a loss are at a higher risk for suffering long-term physical and psychological implications. Scientists use the term *high allostatic load* to refer to this cumulative impact of chronic or repeating stressors across the lifespan, and loss certainly contributes to an elevated load (Guidi et al. 2020).

Considering the contexts in which students' losses occur reminds us to take a step back and appreciate the complexity behind any behavioral changes we see in the classroom. We can then respond to those changes more compassionately while remaining mindful of students' unique needs, too.

Promote Safety, Connection, and Emotional Regulation

Because students' losses are often born out of difficulties beyond teachers' control, it is critical to note that grief is not a problem that teachers should try to fix for their students, but rather a reality to embrace and work through with them. Knowing this, we can take an additive approach to curricular and cocurricular work, asking ourselves, "If we cannot get rid of students' grief or trauma, how—instead—can we supplement and counteract it? What can we facilitate for grieving students? How can we make classroom communities oppositional to the stressful environments that many students—not only those who are grieving—endure beyond school (and, in many cases, at school)? How can we sooth and steady students in times of stress, without pity or placation, while recognizing the systemic intricacies (violence, poverty, inequity, injustice) that may undergird their losses? Can we cultivate resilience rather than teach grit?"

These questions can feel overwhelming for their importance. But we can find tangible strategies by grounding our solution seeking in the three pillars of trauma-informed care: safety, connection, and emotional regulation (Bath 2008). The following definitions offer reference points; you might add on to or alter them yourself.

Safety

Safety is a sense of physical and emotional well-being in which one's basal needs are met or transcended; one has the freedom to express one's identity, experiences, and perspective; and one has the space to take healthy risks, to grow and improve through setbacks.

Connection

Connection is a bond that one has with another person, place, object, or idea; a sense of inclusion and belonging in which one's individuality is both celebrated and meaningfully enmeshed within a larger whole; a reciprocal, attuned energetic exchange that fuels one's sense of well-being.

Emotional Regulation

Emotional regulation is the ability to recognize, reflect on, and process one's internal thoughts and feelings while maintaining mindful control over one's outward actions and reactions.

Leading trauma researcher Bessel van der Kolk, founder of the Trauma Research Foundation and author of *The Body Keeps the Score*, notes that it is only when we immerse our nervous systems in experiences oppositional to trauma that our physiology and psychology can begin to recalibrate and recuperate (2014, 87). A traumatized nervous system, a grieving nervous system, will likely have difficulty learning in any substantive way. We cannot—and should not—remove students' grief, nor imply that they must leave their emotions and experiences in the proverbial hallway. Instead, by supplementing and structuring our classrooms, curricula, and interpersonal relationships with tools for supporting students' sense of safety and connection, and their ability to regulate their emotions, we can create environments supportive of all students' development and learning.

Redirect Risk-Taking Behaviors

The teenage brain is especially vulnerable to the effects of grief and trauma. Because the prefrontal cortex, which controls complex thinking and executive functioning, is still in development, teens' "emotional brains," regulated in part by the amygdala, continue to run the show (Azab 2018). Even though teens lead with their emotional brains, they may become less expressive about their emotional lives. Whereas a five-year-old might experience grief bursts by way of tantrums, meltdowns, or clinginess, teens are more likely to turn to numbing or avoidance mechanisms, suppressing their feelings or channeling them into other outlets (Di Ciacco 2008, 127).

Even without considering for trauma, adolescents are prone to risk-taking; their brains are not fully capable of forethought or impulse control, and these abilities are further diminished in states of grief, stress, and trauma (American Federation of Teachers and New York Life Foundation 2012, 4; Magliano 2015). This means that the outlets teens turn to for relief may involve risk: substance (ab)use, unsafe driving, precarious sexual behaviors, self-harm, and eating disorders, to name a few examples (Nakkula and Toshalis 2006, 42).

But this doesn't have to be the case. School is a critical environment in which students might find a plethora of alternative coping mechanisms and positive risk-taking opportunities that provide control, relief, and community—what students are likely seeking (if subconsciously) when engaging in potentially harmful activities. Grief outlets might look like rugby, rap, meditation, or the debate team. In the chapters to come, activities integrating mindfulness, writing, art, connections with nature, and positive psychology will offer starting points for introducing students to pro-social alternatives to risk-taking behaviors and for building a classroom culture that is supportive of everyone's regulation, teachers' included.

It's particularly important to introduce these alternative behaviors during adolescence because the teenage brain undergoes a period of immense neural development comparable only to that which occurs in the first year and a half of life (Spinks 2002). The brain begins "pruning," or eliminating extra synapses, and the activities and habits of mind teens most frequently engage in determine which synapses remain strong into adulthood (Di Ciacco 2008, 114). The malleability of our brains and our ability to form new neural connections throughout life by changing our behaviors is called *neuroplasticity*, and it is key in our ability to adapt to, and even recover from, early-life adversity.

In a developmental moment when healthy coping mechanisms might restore the body to a state of physiological equilibrium and provide psychological aid throughout the life span, teachers should be on the lookout for students who might benefit from extra encouragement and connect them with new opportunities, redirecting challenging emotions in developmentally appropriate ways.

Empower Students' Awareness of Emotional Regulation

Trauma-informed educators Kristen Souers and Pete Hall write in their book *Fostering Resilient Learners* that students who present challenging behaviors in the classroom (like those listed in Figure 1–2) "are, in essence, having normal responses to not-OK things." "To climb out of survival mode," they tell us, "it is helpful for students to identify the feelings, name the function of their brain, and attune to their biology" (2016, 31).

Teach students about the impact stress has on their brains and bodies by giving them language for the *why* behind their feelings: Introduce the terms *sympathetic nervous system* and *parasympathetic nervous system*, and discuss how both systems influence the way we feel.

1. The sympathetic nervous system controls our fight-or-flight response. When this part of the nervous system is engaged, we feel a fast heartbeat, sweaty palms, tense muscles, quickened breathing. We're ramped up and ready to go or to run away,

depending on our perceived threat. It's hard for our brains to think clearly, let alone learn, while in this state (Harvard Health Publishing 2011).

2. The parasympathetic nervous system is our "rest and digest" system, responsible for making us feel calm and at peace. This is the system we tap into during meditation, yoga, deep breathing, and other relaxation exercises. When we engage our parasympathetic nervous system, we lower our blood pressure, slow our breathing, and create physiological conditions that promote higher cognitive functioning (van der Kolk 2014, 79; Shulman 2018, 95).

A common metaphor for understanding the sympathetic and parasympathetic nervous systems comes from trauma scientist Dan Siegel, who describes the former as the "downstairs brain" and the latter as "the upstairs brain" (Souers and Hall 2016, 31). In our upstairs brain, we engage in executive functioning—reasoning, analyzing, thinking, learning, planning, dreaming, imagining, inhibiting impulses. But grief, stress, and trauma throw us into our downstairs brain, which makes it quite challenging to achieve any of these tasks.

Both our upstairs and downstairs brains are crucial to survival. They carry their own unique wisdom, alerting us to situations that are, in Souers and Hall's words, "not-OK." When working with teens, it's important to emphasize that the downstairs brain is not bad, nor is the upstairs brain ideal. We need to listen to and integrate both.

Sometimes, though, the downstairs brain overdoes it. It can be perfectionistic and doesn't always know when it's time to leave the party. When this happens, and the sympathetic nervous system is stuck in overdrive, students might exhibit the behaviors outlined in Figure 1–2. In such moments, it's helpful for both students and teachers to have strategies on hand to promote self-regulation and de-escalation. These strategies might look different for every student, especially because the behaviors born out of the downstairs brain occur on a broad spectrum, but there are a number of ways we can all work to access our upstairs brain when we're feeling stuck in our brain basement, each strategy a rung of the ladder.

To help students identify ways they can access their upstairs brain, even in times of stress, ask them to create three columns on a piece of paper and label the columns "Upstairs Brain," "Downstairs Brain," and "Tool Kit." In the first two columns, invite students to list bullet points describing how their minds and bodies feel in these states. In the final column, ask them to reflect on activities they find relaxing—things they can turn to the next time they need to access their upstairs brain. With a younger group (grades 6–9), you might invite students to draw a diagram of a "brain building," such as the one in Figure 1–3, to further reinforce Siegel's metaphor.

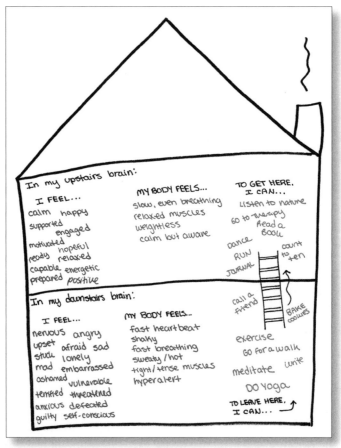

Figure 1–3   Brain Building Drawing

Write and Reflect

Write about a time when you were teaching from your upstairs brain—tuned in, focused, immersed in the moment of learning. Re-create that scene on the page using sensory details, dialogue, description; immerse yourself in that memory.

Next, write about a time when you were teaching from your downstairs brain—perhaps distracted by a personal loss or conflict or struggling to calibrate to a student's challenging behaviors. Re-create the scene, using vivid details in vignette form.

Now, take a few minutes to complete these exercises again with students in mind. When in your career has a student notably and noticeably come into class using their downstairs brain? How about upstairs? What did those interactions sound, look, and feel like?

Compare the scenes you've created. What do they teach you? How can you gain greater distance from students' downstairs brain behaviors? What helps you take a responsive rather than reactive approach? If you were to create your own brain building diagram, what strategies would you list as helpful regulators? Where do you turn in times of stress? List five examples.

CHAPTER

2

What Should I Do?
How Can I Help?

A Protocol for Action

*One looks back with appreciation to the
brilliant teachers, but with gratitude to
those who touched our human feelings.
The curriculum is so much necessary raw
material, but warmth is the vital element
for the growing plant and for the soul of
the child.*

—*CARL JUNG,* THE DEVELOPMENT OF PERSONALITY

It was 2005. Velada Chaires was new to Springfield Central High School, where she joined the staff as an adjustment counselor, bringing with her the knowledge that she had cultivated while earning her master of social work degree at Smith College and working in a jail system. She was settling into her office in the library, acclimating to the demands of working within the second largest school district in the state of Massachusetts (public, urban, with 90 percent of graduates headed for college [Springfield Public Schools 2017]) when she was met with crisis—forced to, as she said, "learn by fire."

The hallways at Central filled with boys who were "crying and hitting things," running out of classrooms as a wave washed over the building: a senior and star basketball player, we'll call him Jerome, had been shot and killed in a drive-by. His friends were stunned. His teachers were devastated. To Velada's recollection, police officials never caught the shooter.

"I quickly figured out that I needed help," Velada told me, recalling the incident.

> We had to call in community people to help us manage the boys, because they were angry. Everything about them was just angry. It was the first time I ever saw prayer in school—an entire community came in and prayed with the boys. And then [we] had to separate the groups. The basketball team was one group, and the cheerleaders were a different group. The kids who had him in class . . . the kids who thought they knew him and thought they should be affected. The contagion was crazy. When that kind of stuff happens, it can be so unmanageable, and . . . it fell on me. There were just so many layers.

Faced with acute grief on a large scale—a communal "contagion"—Velada spoke with her supervisor and school administrators to galvanize the creation of a crisis response team that continues to operate today. Because she recognized resistance and reticence among students when school staff members sought to support them, she envisioned this external team as a cohort of "people who could talk to [the boys] and people [whom] they felt comfortable talking to"—therapists, trained responders, and community mentors with whom the student body could identify.

I sat with Velada in Springfield, at a sunny Starbucks picnic table, on her first day of the 2019–20 school year, fourteen years after this tragedy occurred. "It was too big," she told me over the whir of interstate traffic.

> It took over the building. No work got done for four days. . . . I had to start learning how to figure out which kids really needed more [support], which kids just needed to get through, which kids were the 'hanger-oners', who had parents that could help them. Kids were coming to school; they weren't staying home. They were coming in just to cry.
>
> That was the first big introduction to crisis work for me. I used to work in the jail, and coming from the jail system to that, it was a very different beast, because the jail is very controlled. School is not—it's fluid. You had to improvise all the time. And there was also a safety issue, because there were kids who knew him, and you didn't know if those kids were going to be safe in the street. It was hard to figure out, because it wasn't something that I knew about.

Here Be Dragons: Tools for Uncharted Territory

Loss may slip into the life of a student or schooling community quietly. Other times, as at Velada's school, grief disrupts as a lightning bolt to the building. In both instances, emotion can muddy our thinking, the size and scope of loss rendering action elusive or unclear. As ancient topographers noted uncharted territory with the infamous phrase, "Here Be Dragons," so can grief work feel foreign.

I resist condensing grief support into steps or tutorials, lest that framework reduce the complexity of the work to an inappropriately simplistic (or misleadingly standardized) form. However, when the presence of loss at school feels just too big, and teachers' decisions in the wake of it could create or negate a safe space, there is calm to be found in the certitude of a checklist or procedure to turn to for guidance. Science writer Atul Gawande, who writes elegantly about mortality and medicine, describes good checklists as "practical," adding: "They do not try to spell out everything. . . . Instead, they provide reminders of only the most critical and important steps—the ones that even the highly skilled professional using them could miss" (2010, 120). This chapter offers distilled checklists to follow in the midst of loss experiences that impact individual students as well as those that challenge school systems at large. Consider them your gentle reminders. Your critical and important steps. Your starting place.

When Loss Impacts a Student

During my first semester studying education in college, I completed a multicultural education practicum in a local fourth-grade classroom, where I spent most of my time poring over literacy worksheets with a struggling but tenacious reader. We sharpened our pencils together and stuck with the tricky task of sentence construction, celebrating our progress along the way. This was a boy who was beloved by his classmates. His humor was ever present, his giggle contagious. But during our time together, he showed me a serious side. He voiced doubt in himself and his work. He dropped his pencil midsentence, saying, "I don't know," and looked to me for answers. I could see that, beneath this student's jokes, there was an unsure but hopeful reader, and I could not imagine a better pairing, for I was an unsure but hopeful educator. We helped each other, in this way—he teaching me how to teach, I teaching him how to trust himself.

Immersed as I was in these tutoring sessions, I felt my attention being tugged by one corner of the classroom that held an empty chair—blue, with tennis balls on its feet. A student, I'll call her Anna, was usually seated there, smiling behind black, thick-rimmed glasses. Lately, however, she was in school less frequently than before, and her absence changed the feel of the room.

As I entered the classroom one morning, Anna's teacher pulled me aside to tell me that Anna's mother had died from a terminal illness. The loss was expected but devastating.

Soon, Anna returned to school for half days, then full days, with the agreement that she could go home if she needed to. She had a younger brother in kindergarten, who clung to her legs when he saw her in the hallway, begging her not to leave—at times on the verge of tears.

My heart broke for Anna as I watched her care for and comfort her sibling in the wing of the school—and as I watched her father pick her up around noon, slinging her peace-sign backpack over his shoulder, his son perched on his hip. The image in my mind of the three of them, engaged in quotidian routine just weeks after their mother's and wife's death, serves for me as a humbling reminder of the ways in which insular loss—impacting a student or family—reverberates throughout a schooling community, the reciprocal relationship between students' and teachers' lives rendering an altered milieu.

Over the course of the term, Anna's relationship with her teacher blossomed. The two had an intimate bond that made me smile as I watched from the side. But I'm sure that it took time to get to that space. Relationships are not often built in one day; trust and rapport are strata of interactions and experiences, built layer-by-layer over time.

Knowing that I, too, experienced the death of a parent during my time as a student, Anna's teacher approached me with an idea. She had a book comprising chapters written by bereaved children and teens and wondered if I might give it a read to see if I thought it would prove helpful for Anna.

I welcomed the opportunity and admired this teacher's sincerity. She was determined to create a classroom space in which Anna felt validated and welcomed. She wanted to be a person to whom Anna could turn, and she had the forethought to be intentional about her relational approach. Leafing through the pages of this text in my dorm room one weekend, however, I happened upon chapters in which children divulged their deepest fears—how they worried about their parents remarrying or moving, how they were surprised to love new stepmothers and stepfathers.

Returning to Anna's classroom on Monday, I shared my concern with her teacher. Some of the stories were lovely and may very well aid Anna by making her feel less alone; however, I worried that other narratives may incite fears in her, especially at this early stage of her grieving process. What if she hadn't yet thought about the possibility of her father remarrying? What if the thought caused her deep anxiety?

Anna's teacher let out a gasp when I said this. "Of course!" she exclaimed, wide-eyed. "How come I didn't think of that?!"

Later in this book, we will talk about moments of repair—what Anna's teacher could have done, for instance, had she gifted this text to Anna and later realized its potential pitfalls. But for now, this memory seems a relevant example of the ways in which wonderful intentions and a willingness to directly address students' grief experiences are not foolproof precursors to dodging the creaky boards in the bridge of student support. When loss impacts a student or family, the steps in Figure 2–1 (also available as Online Resource 2–1) offer actionable guidance throughout the progression of grief; "they do not try to spell out everything," to Gawande's point (2010, 120), but are instead porous suggestions—"fluid," as Velada would say. The possibility of alteration and rearrangement, as well as room for repair, is always at your fingertips.

Check in with yourself. Choose the space from which you respond to a student's loss.

Many of us react to grief from a place of fear, anger, denial, or judgment, but we often do so passively or because our prior life experiences have conditioned us to do so. We can instead elect to react from a place of presence, centeredness, and care, even if those around us are struggling to do so, but we first must check in with our feelings and reactions and consider the why behind them. What do you notice about your own response to grief and loss? What has led you to have that reaction? As you process your own positioning, return to the intentions you set at the start of this book, and keep them in mind as you initiate contact with a grieving student in your classroom.

Map out a personal-care plan.

Supporting grieving students is challenging work, especially when their grief can raise thoughts and feelings about our own fears, losses, and traumas. Using a personal-care permission slip (see Chapter 5) as a guide, consider these questions: Whom in your circle of family, friends, and colleagues can you turn to for support and conversation? Who knows how best to listen to you? Are there

Grief Checklist: Student-Centric Loss

- ☐ Check in with yourself. Choose the space from which you respond to a student's loss.

- ☐ Map out a personal-care plan.

- ☐ Communicate with the impacted student.

- ☐ Collaborate with the student, as well as family members if appropriate, to address classroom accommodations.

- ☐ Prioritize the student's privacy and preferences.

- ☐ Notice how students and colleagues communicate about loss.

- ☐ Regulate routine in the classroom.

- ☐ Cull curricula; create teaching and trigger plans.

- ☐ Call upon and collaborate with specialists and resources.

- ☐ Follow up with the grieving student and maintain open communication across time.

Figure 2-1   Grief Checklist: Student-Centric Loss

professionals whom you feel comfortable turning to? Secondly, make a list of activities that help you destress and reregulate (e.g., running, cooking, yoga). Set parameters around your work life to afford distance and space so that you can maintain your own well-being in the face of grief work. Doing this from the outset lays a foundation for success in supporting grieving students.

Communicate with the impacted student.

Using the CODE framework addressed in Chapter 4, open a conversation with the impacted student. Express authentic concern, and use open-ended questions that encourage students to tell you about their lived experience to the extent that feels comfortable to them. Don't force disclosure, but do ask students how you can best support them, and establish a plan together regarding any classroom needs. In this initial conversation, position yourself as a member on this student's team, and ask them about their wishes: Do they want other students and teachers to know about the loss? If so, would they like to share the news themselves, or would they prefer that you share the news with specified individuals? Your directives will often become clear from direct communications with the impacted student.

Collaborate with the student, as well as family members if appropriate, to address classroom accommodations.

Grieving students may need an adjusted workload, with a gradual ascension or reintegration into classroom life. They may also benefit from more frequent brain breaks throughout the day; the opportunity to connect with the school counselor or a trusted teacher or friend; or the option to call home during the days following a loss. Work together with the student to put a plan in place for how you can best support what they're going through while also maintaining structure, routine, and the healthy expectations that we know to be helpful during times of stress.

Prioritize the student's privacy and preferences.

It's important to respect students' and families' privacy and preferences when learning about, and potentially speaking with others about, their loss. Because trust and safety are foundational in the creation of a grief-responsive environment, communicate directly with the affected student first, as well as their family member(s) if appropriate, before sharing their loss story with colleagues and administrators.

Depending on the circumstance, it may feel appropriate to apprise others of a student's story—the school counselor, for example, or a colleague who is also interacting with the student, especially if concern arises regarding the student's well-being. Be mindful that you pay heed to students' wishes whenever possible; for example, invite them to share their story with others in their own words. The urge to share the story of a student's loss may come from a place of caring, but it will be counterproductive if a student arrives at school to discover you've spread their story without permission. Turn to support staff for suggestions about how best to navigate loss in your professional role, but only disclose specific details about a student's story when absolutely essential (or when withholding information would violate your duties as a mandated reporter).

Notice how students and colleagues communicate about loss.

Take note of the grief climate in which you find yourself working. When a loss impacts your learning environment, how do those around you respond? Do others seem open to discussing loss; make caustic jokes and judgmental comparisons; or perhaps go on with business as usual without addressing the issue at all? Know that you don't need to change others' reactions, but pay attention to the tendencies you witness and stay aware of how others' reactions in-fluence your own approach and attitude toward grief work. Chances are, grieving students will pick up on the attitudes of others, so scanning your professional environment in this way will allow you to glean insight into the messages and energy your students may be internalizing, which can in turn inform your intentional response.

Regulate routine in the classroom.

Reflect upon how you already structure routine in your classroom—the expectations, activities, or processes that stay the same each day, week, or month. Next, consider how you can further support consistency and dependability in grieving students' lives: How can you offer them a sense of control in the classroom—for example, through activities that afford them choice and agency—to offset the turmoil and upheaval of loss? How might you institute regular check-ins with them, creating a sense of predictability around social-emotional support?

Cull curricula; create teaching and trigger plans (Coalition to Support Grieving Students n.d.).

Scan your syllabus for curricular material that may raise challenging feelings for students who are going through grief. Check in with those students about their thoughts, feelings, and comfort levels regarding this proposed material. Offer alternative texts or topics of study to differentiate instruction, and confer with them in a calm moment to put together a plan for times when hard feelings might arise in response to curricular content: stake out a space where they can go, for example, if they feel activated; identify a person they can talk to; and name an activity they can do when feeling sad, scared, or dysregulated. To guide this conversation, you can use the personal-care permission slip provided in Chapter 5.

Know that reading and writing about loss can sometimes facilitate healing, and it's impossible to avoid challenging topics in academic content. The goal here is not to avoid reality so much as to scaffold curricular engagement by empowering students to take a challenge-by-choice approach.

Call upon and collaborate with specialists and resources.

Identify support resources available to you in and outside of your school system. At the micro level, do you have access to a school psychologist, nurse, counselor, or administrator? In your local community, can you connect with grief counselors, grief support groups or organizations, social workers, psychologists, therapists, or professional development groups? In the broader community, what resources can you consult (e.g., professional organizations, helplines, websites, books, journals, webinars)? List three resources you can turn to.

*Follow up with the grieving student and
maintain open communication across time.*

We know that grief does not have a set end point, and students may struggle with a loss long after they let on anything is wrong. For that reason, keep your communication with a grieving student open; check in with them periodically, and consider how you might provide ongoing mentoring or support, even if they don't make disclosures to you about their grief. Know that consistency and connection are great antidotes to adversity, and your relationship with a grieving student can be a buffer that supports their well-being.

When Loss Impacts a School

Glenn Manning, a prior high school English teacher who is now the senior program coordinator at Making Caring Common, a social-emotional learning initiative sponsored by Harvard University's Graduate School of Education, spoke to me about his experiences with teaching in a district that was going through communal loss. "The district in which I was teaching unfortunately suffered a number of student suicides—several seniors [and] one student very, very tragically in fifth grade," he shared.

> The year really shook the community, and that was a devas-
> tating time for everyone. It really didn't matter if the teachers
> knew those students or their families. It impacted everybody—
> obviously differently, but there was a palpable sense of loss
> and it was really scary for a lot of our students, and a lot of
> people who felt chiefly responsible for their well-being and
> their safety. It really impacted me on a personal level.

Glenn's background in social-emotional learning afforded him unique insight into the challenges and potentials of scaffolding grief work with students. He noted that a primary focus of that work was attending to "caring relationships" between students, faculty, and staff. The term reminded me of Marjory Stoneman Douglas High School in Parkland, Florida, where—on Valentine's Day in 2018—an active shooter took the lives of seventeen people and traumatized countless others. It sickens and sobers me when reading articles recapping this tragedy, imagining the challenges that surviving community members continue to face because of this senseless act. Here, too, caring relationships took priority and fueled action toward change. To return to dance teacher Laurel Boyd's words, the people facing these crises sought not to "lose the dancer for the dance," banding together—as in Velada's school—to support young people, as well as each other, as they sat with the incomprehensible.

There is much similarity, but also some difference, between loss protocols for grief that impacts a student and grief that affects a wider school community. When you take a look at Figure 2–2 (also available as Online Resource 2–2), you'll notice many familiar suggestions as well as greater emphases on certain aspects (memorialization, individualization) that gain heightened importance when dealing with loss on a larger scale and tending to caring relationships amid crisis.

Check in with yourself. Choose the space from which you respond to the loss.

As noted in the previous section, many of us react to grief from a place of fear, anger, denial, or judgment, but we often do so passively or because we've been conditioned to do so. We can instead elect to react from a place of presence, centeredness, and care, even if those around us are struggling to do so, but making such a choice can feel extra challenging when loss impacts a school, because we are most likely grieving alongside our students. Check in with yourself regularly: What do you notice about your own response to grief and loss? What has led you to have that reaction? Are you receiving the support you need? As you process your own positioning, return to the intentions you set at the start of this book, and keep them in mind as you initiate contact with grieving students in your classroom. Share your intentions with colleagues and students if you feel inclined; doing so will create space for communication about your shared loss.

Map out a personal-care plan.

Supporting grieving students is challenging work, especially when you may also be grieving. Using a personal-care permission slip (Chapter 5) as a guide, consider these questions: Whom in your circle of family, friends, and colleagues can you turn to for support and conversation? Who knows how best to listen to you? Are there professionals whom you feel comfortable turning to? Secondly, make a list of activities that help you destress and reregulate (e.g., running, cooking, yoga). Set parameters around your work life to afford distance and space so that you can maintain your own well-being in the face of grief work.

Communicate with administrators and crisis response professionals (as applicable) about any schoolwide action plan and how you can implement it in your classroom.

When loss impacts a school, there is often a protocol imposed upon teachers by administrators or outside specialists who are called in to offer their advice. Pay attention to any directives given, and consider how you can enact schoolwide protocols while also tailoring your supportive approach to meet what you know to be the needs of your students.

Connect with colleagues. Notice how others react to and talk about the event.

Take note of the grief climate in which you find yourself working, especially when your colleagues may also be grieving. Do others seem open to discussing the loss and their approach to supporting students? Do they make caustic jokes and judgmental comparisons or perhaps go on with business as usual and neglect to address the issue at all? Are they overly positive, insisting on putting an optimistic spin on the tragedy that took place? Know that you don't need to change others' reactions, but pay attention to the tendencies you witness and stay aware of how others' reactions influence your own approach and attitude toward grief work. Chances are, grieving students will pick up on the attitudes of others, so scanning your professional environment in this way will allow you to glean insight into the messages and energy they may be internalizing, which can in turn inform your intentional response.

Grief Checklist: School-Centric Loss

- ☐ Check in with yourself. Choose the space from which you respond to the loss.
- ☐ Map out a personal-care plan.
- ☐ Communicate with administrators and crisis response professionals (as applicable) about any schoolwide action plan and how you can implement it in your classroom.
- ☐ Connect with colleagues. Notice how others react to and talk about the event.
- ☐ Speak with students and family members about the event and your response.
- ☐ Adjust workload as appropriate.
- ☐ Identify and watch out for students for whom loss or trauma may prove especially challenging.
- ☐ Make space for multimodal communication or expression about the event within your classroom and caring relationships.
- ☐ Regulate routine in your classroom to the extent that is possible. Support a sense of safety at school.
- ☐ Consider collective memorialization efforts (schoolwide, classwide) to execute with your students.
- ☐ Cull curricular content; create a grief trigger plan.
- ☐ Call upon and collaborate with specialists and resources.
- ☐ Continue the conversation.

Figure 2–2: Grief Checklist: School-Centric Loss

Speak with students and family members about the event and your response.

Be transparent with students and their family members about the school-based loss experience and your response to it in the classroom. You might talk about any schoolwide approaches that you and your colleagues have undertaken while emphasizing your individual efforts to create safety, connection, and an environment supportive of emotional regulation in your learning space. Welcome their questions and maintain a reciprocal dialogue in the aftermath of the loss.

Adjust workload as appropriate.

Students who are grieving deserve accommodations, and they also often benefit from routine, structure, and healthy expectations. Collaborate with colleagues to integrate any schoolwide accommodations in your classroom; if none exist, create an approach that works for you and your students, knowing that they will most likely benefit from a flexible workload and gradual ascension or reintegration into the classroom in the period following a loss. Because some grieving students may throw themselves into work for distraction, you should also consider how best to support balance in the lives of your students.

Identify and watch out for students for whom loss or trauma may prove especially challenging.

Students who have a history of trauma or grief may prove especially vulnerable to, or have an attenuated ability to cope with, loss. Think about the composition of your classroom. Do you have students who you know have endured loss? How about homelessness, foster care, or a parent who struggles with addiction? Are there children in your room who have lived through a natural disaster or who have a parent overseas in the military? Are there students who have experienced a house fire? Students who struggle to self-regulate? Keep a careful eye on these students. Think about their unique needs and what you already know about the learning and communication styles that click for them. Alter your support strategies according to your history with these students, realizing that the strength already required of them can make it more challenging for them to face loss at school.

*Make space for multimodal communication
or expression about the event within your
classroom and caring relationships.*

Talking about loss is challenging for all of us and may prove out
of reach for some students. Be sure that, in your efforts to support
grief work, students have opportunities to express themselves in a
multitude of ways: writing, drawing, advocating, fundraising, creating, running, dancing, and meditating are all ways for students to
find the space and awareness to work through tough times and their
responses to them.

*Regulate routine in your classroom to the extent that
is possible. Support a sense of safety at school.*

Reflect upon how you already structure routine in your classroom—
the expectations, activities, or processes that stay the same each
day, week, or month. Next, consider how you can further support
consistency and dependability in grieving students' lives: How can
you offer them a sense of control in the classroom—for example,
through activities that afford them choice and agency—to offset
the turmoil and upheaval of loss? Deaths that impact a schooling
community may involve violence or severe illness, and they can
incite fear in students of all ages. Jot down some interventions you
might incorporate into your daily classroom routine to assuage
students' anxieties, such as meditation, sharing circles, dedicated
spaces or times to come together and speak about the event, or other
community-building activities.

*Consider collective memorialization efforts (schoolwide,
classwide) to execute with your students.*

In Chapter 7, we'll explore the importance of communal memorialization. Consider the nature of your and your students' relationship with the deceased and students' wishes and ideas about how
to honor their legacy. What feels within reach for you to facilitate?
How can your classroom community heal and grow together through
memorialization efforts?

Cull curricular content; create a grief trigger plan (Coalition to Support Grieving Students n.d.).

Scanning your syllabus for curricular material that may raise challenging feelings for students who are going through grief is even more important when loss impacts a school. Check in with students regarding their thoughts, feelings, and comfort levels regarding proposed material, and keep in mind any outside guidance you receive from administrators or support professionals regarding challenging content.

Consider offering alternative texts or topics of study to differentiate instruction for students, and confer with them in a calm moment to put together a plan for times when hard feelings might arise: stake out a space where they can go, for example, if they feel activated; identify a person they can talk to; and name an activity they can do when feeling sad, scared, or dysregulated. To guide this conversation, you can use the personal-care permission slip provided in Chapter 5.

Know that reading and writing about loss can sometimes facilitate healing, and it's impossible to avoid challenging topics in academic content. The goal here is not to avoid reality so much as to scaffold curricular engagement by empowering students to take a challenge-by-choice approach.

Call upon and collaborate with specialists and resources.

Identify support resources available to you in and outside of your school system. At the micro level, do you have access to a school psychologist, nurse, counselor, or administrator? In your local community, can you connect with grief counselors, grief support groups or organizations, social workers, psychologists, therapists, or professional development communities? In the broader community, what resources can you consult (e.g., professional organizations, helplines, websites, books, journals, webinars)? List three resources you can turn to.

Continue the conversation.

Grief that impacts a school community can disrupt the learning environment beyond one academic year. Keep your communication with grieving students and colleagues open; check in with them periodically, and consider how you might provide and seek ongoing support. Know that consistency and connection are great antidotes to adversity, and your relationship with grieving students and colleagues can be a buffer that supports well-being. Yet you, too, need continued connection and support and should not feel shy about seeking out resources even after the visible aftermath of a loss concludes.

Throughout this book, we will explore the specifics of many of these checkpoints, from communicating with students and parents while sustaining ongoing mentoring (Chapter 4) to approaching mortality and content warnings in curricula (Chapter 5). I encourage you to return to these checklists throughout your reading experience, carrying with you new knowledge, experiences, and questions.

The Importance of Energy over Directives

As helpful as it is to turn to instructions in times of vulnerability, following any strictures too closely can also breed anxiety or imply that there is a right and wrong way to approach loss, which often is not the case. Following loss, whether at the individual or communal level, focus on the feeling—rather than the procedure—with which you hope to structure students' schooling experiences. Students are likely to respond viscerally to a teacher exuding warmth and willingness, or fear and frustration, no matter the words that come out of that teacher's mouth. "Many students are especially sensitive to the emotional energy in a classroom," writes Jane Bluestein in *Creating Emotionally Safe Schools*, "particularly that which is subtly broadcast by the teacher's emotional state. These students can sense tension, impatience and hostility, or enthusiasm, delight or calm in others, and may be particularly adept if they come from a background of trauma or abuse, where this hypervigilance is a practiced survival skill" (2001, 25).

Of course, such an emotional state is—to an extent—ineffable. It does not equate with the effeminate, Pollyanna nature that may come to mind but rather an authenticity and honesty in action and reaction that requires careful calibration. Children crave honesty. And students of all ages can read into our receptivity and sincerity. They may even tend toward "a negativity bias," as Laurel mentioned during our interview, especially if they have experienced trauma, which alters brain structures implicated in negative self-perception (van der Kolk 2000; Slaninova and Stainerova 2015). Laurel explained,

> I think a lot of times for students, especially in the teenage years, there can be a negativity bias. It can feel for students a lot like it's us versus them, teachers versus students, a strangely adversarial relationship in some ways. I always have questions about the right way to approach. I've always felt pretty confident that if I at least let them know that I see they're going through something and that I care, I find that, more often than not, over time, they'll be able to share a little bit of it. But the key is to deliver that message consistently.

Part of "delivering that message consistently" means maintaining awareness of tacit communication—the messages that we send to students and colleagues through our body language, eye contact, and other nonverbal cues. In your interactions with grieving students, ask yourself: What message is my body language communicating to this student, and does that message align with my intent? Am I making eye contact with this young person? Are my nonverbal cues creating a calm environment supportive of their expression?

What we say to students will lose its impact if our actions and nonverbal communications misalign with our spoken messages. Creating a classroom environment that feels safe and secure in the context of grief, no matter the scale, begins with you, the educator, whose actions reverberate outward to students and colleagues in your community and beyond. This is an area where it's important to check in with yourself, too—if you find it challenging to create a calm environment through your nonverbal cues, it likely means that you have your own work to do regarding the topic, story, or situation at hand, and that is OK. When we come to this realization, we can adjust our approach to students by connecting them with a colleague or professional who is better equipped to tackle a certain topic, or by addressing student support from a different angle. Self-awareness allows us to recognize that the space we create with and for students impacts how they feel about themselves and their stories, and to calibrate our work accordingly.

Write and Reflect

What thoughts, questions, fears, and hopes come to mind when you think about teaching students who are grieving? What do you feel toward these students? What do you wonder? Honor your first thoughts without judgment.

3

Where Should I Start?

Creating Safety in the Classroom

"I am one of those who like to stay late at the café," the older waiter said. "With all those who do not want to go to bed. With all those who need a light for the night. . . ."

"It is not only a question of youth and confidence although those things are very beautiful. Each night I am reluctant to close up because there may be someone who needs the café."

—ERNEST HEMINGWAY, "A CLEAN WELL-LIGHTED PLACE"

Children learn early on, either consciously or unconsciously, ways to stay safe, to attempt to control their surroundings, and to manage their stress levels. . . . Often, constructing a "tornado" is just a learned tactic of avoiding the truth.

—KRISTEN SOUERS AND PETE HALL, FOSTERING RESILIENT LEARNERS

Some Reflections on Safety

When I study grief literature, as well as its intersections with childhood trauma and adverse childhood experiences (ACEs), I picture my father's childhood. He grew up in a ramshackle apartment that is now a parking lot, in extreme poverty, at times without food. His mother was chronically ill and unable to work; his divorced father battled alcoholism and, with his new wife, abused my father and his four siblings physically and verbally. For my dad, summer vacations meant spending daytimes locked outside, with PB and J sandwiches placed on a cement stoop for lunch.

It seemed like unreality, hearing his stories as a child. I could relate only to his tales of playing kick the can with his buddies and biking around town with a baseball mitt in his basket. Home, for me, was gentle and kind, for my father found parenting redemptive. His ACE score would have been at least a seven, yet evidence of his past, and any scars that lingered from it, did not manifest before my eyes except in the form of love.

I'm sure that the story ran deeper. Now, I would ask so many questions: *What sustained you? What haunts you? How did you keep from getting stuck (in trauma, in pain, in grief for what could have been)?*

I am conscious of the ways in which my father's identity as a white, heterosexual, able-bodied man in Western Massachusetts contributed to his attaining the upward mobility that facilitated my own childhood. Surely, he had grit and resilience and the character strengths that imbue social-emotional learning literature. However, he also had sociopolitical privilege as leverage. Had he grown up in a different city, with a different name, racial identity, physical ability, or other marginalized identifier, he may not have transcended his circumstances in quite the same way. He may not have transcended them at all.

My father also had social support. Safety, for him, was found on the banks of a rushing river at his grandmother's house. On the other side of town, she and her husband settled into a small home on an even smaller plot of land, relocating from New York after their daughter's divorce. Unable to financially or physically take care of five children, they knew that they could not fix my father's circumstances, nor those of his siblings, but they could provide peripheral support. My father could escape for tea and scones on their back porch and cast fishing rods in the rapids.

I have driven past this abode by the river. It is rusty, rundown, smaller than I ever imagined—so grand are the stories that surround it. I can, however, hear the rush of water hitting the same craggy banks. I can picture my mother and father, in love, finding solace among the rocks. It makes sense, listening to the water with my windows rolled down, that safety is not only physical.

We need food, water, shelter—sure—but also love and attention. We need witnesses who understand the gravity of our challenges and the thrill of our accomplishments. We need people who can believe us into being.*

For me, the story of my great-grandparents is an example not only of physical refuge—a home, a stove, food in the pantry—but of the salve that presence can provide in the lives of people who are struggling. The disparity between their house's reality and the happiness that it gave way to is testament to the role of antidotal support. My great-grandmother Hillman knew her limits; she could not fix my father's life—take him in, offer monetary resources—but she could love him from the side. She could be a positive, encouraging force in his life. And for him, that made a tremendous difference.

So it is that we need to understand both the physical and emotional subsets of safety to lay the foundation for grief work—and students' holistic well-being—at school. We must keep in mind that teachers can provide peripheral protection against life's blows, simply by sharing presence. You need not fix or take hold of students' struggles. Velada Chaires told me, "You can't take them home. You have to remember that you can't take them home." But, within

---

*When I first wrote this line, I turned it over and over in my mind, feeling like I'd heard it before. Numerous searches garnered no source, but one year later, I sat down to watch *A Beautiful Day in the Neighborhood* and, at long last, happened upon its origins. Fred Rogers asked adults—in his 1997 Emmy Award acceptance speech (available on YouTube) and elsewhere—to pause for sixty seconds of silence and think of all the people "who loved [them] into being." I offer the adapted line here and the suggestion that you practice this activity by yourself and with students, as simply calling to mind social support can prove beneficial in times of loss.

the classroom and educational jurisdiction, there is much that people and pedagogies can do to support grieving students within appropriate professional and interpersonal bounds.

Physical Safety

Physical safety is the primary priority when supporting young learners, especially those who are dealing with grief or trauma. It will come as no surprise that students who are facing a lack of physical safety at home—gun violence, physical abuse, hunger, homelessness—often rely, consciously or subconsciously, on the classroom for stability, even if their behaviors in the classroom challenge this supposition at times. The same holds true for students who are grieving. Jana DeCristofaro, licensed clinical social worker and community response program coordinator at the Dougy Center, the National Grief Center for Children and Families, told me about the security that teachers can provide in times of tumult by incorporating "predictability, routine, and consistency" into students' days:

> A lot of times, for kids, coming to school maybe isn't the place where they want to be doing a lot of emotional work. It's their safe refuge where they can come and know where they sit, what the expectations are, how the day is going to start and end. Building in routine in the classroom can be really helpful and supportive for all kids who are going through challenging, stressful times in their [lives].

Of course, not all classrooms are physically safe, even when they seem to be—for example, Parkland, Florida, ranked as one of the safest cities just months before the 2017 shooting at Marjory Stoneman Douglas (Reilly 2018). Bullying and peer-to-peer violence can present additional threats, both emotional and physical. And in some school districts, often those that are most underfunded, whether urban or rural, the very buildings in which teachers and students gather can present health hazards (Bluestein 2001, 315).

Within your immediate control is the extent to which you cater to (and transcend) Maslow's hierarchy of needs in your learning environment by imparting to students a sense of physical safety through the "predictability, routine, and consistency" that you scaffold within the classroom (McLeod 2020). Schoolwide resources are also important (subsidized lunch programs, quiet rooms where students can go for a break, etc.). But, while children are in your room, you can take the following steps:

- Begin and end class periods in the same way each day; for example, by starting each class session with a mindfulness activity or closing with a freewriting-based exit ticket.

- Set up scheduled check-ins with students at the same time each day or week.

- Make students aware of their daily schedule at the outset, offering a heads-up if there will be a break in routine.

"I talk about how kids crave that sense of safety that the classroom provides," affirmed Shelly Bathe Lenn, who is the bereavement coordinator for Cooley Dickinson Hospital VNA and Hospice and the Garden, a center for grieving children and teens affiliated with Cooley Dickinson Hospital in Northampton, Massachusetts. She was speaking about the professional development sessions that she leads for teachers and parents, bringing her knowledge as a grief support specialist to local school districts. "That doesn't mean that they're all there cognitively," she added. "You may see them in your classroom, but that doesn't mean they're following you, or that their mind isn't thinking about the death. For some, they're ruminating over what happened, what they thought they saw, what they thought they heard, what they did hear, and replaying it over and over in their head."

No matter how small a schedule might seem, a classroom structured around consistency can support students' regulation as they navigate this potential rumination, regain their footing, and work toward resiliency in the face of grief.

Emotional Safety

The term *social-emotional learning* is relatively new in the educational sphere, dating back only to 1994. However, the ideas embedded within the methodology—defined by the Collaborative for Academic, Social, and Emotional Learning (CASEL) as "the

Pause and Plan

Jot down, in whatever format works for you (bulleted list, paragraph) strategies you already use to establish routine and consistency in your classroom. Then, take a look at your list and consider these questions: What are three additional ways you can scaffold consistency and constancy for students who are grieving? What will you need to do to put these strategies into action? What changes will you make? What challenges might you face? Put down an action plan.

process through which all young people and adults acquire and apply the knowledge, skills and attitudes to develop healthy identities, manage emotions and achieve personal and collective goals, feel and show empathy for others, establish and maintain supportive relationships, and make responsible and caring decisions" (2021)—are not new. Even Plato's *The Republic* broached the possibility of a curriculum that included character and moral judgment alongside traditional subject matter and physical education (Edutopia 2011).

In Western culture, there seems a degree of consensus that teaching and learning must transcend textbook knowledge—the transactional model that Paulo Freire admonishes in *Pedagogy of the Oppressed* (1970). We realize that the tenets of social-emotional learning and character development—empathy, impulse control, positive relationality, resilience—contribute to and depend upon a sense of emotional safety in the classroom and fuel students' happiness and success outside of the classroom, across their life span. There is such energy around this idea, in fact, that over forty frameworks (and counting) exist to implement and measure programming that promotes social-emotional learning at and beyond school (EASEL Lab n.d.).

You can cultivate emotional safety in the classroom through your own social-emotional competencies, which I refer to as the three Rs of grief support: how you *recognize*, *respect*, and *respond* to grieving students' presence in the classroom (especially when that presence may manifest as cognitive-behavioral challenges) not only fosters a sense of safety for all students but determines the extent to which safety transcends physical logistics and connects with teachers' and students' emotional lives, the psychosocial setting of the classroom. "There are myriad ways in which schools can and should support students," former high school teacher Glenn Manning told me when we spoke about his losing students to suicide. "Before we suffered those tragedies, we attempted to put in place not only the kind of acute support, counseling department, SOS, trauma-response type of work but also the supportive relationships . . . the scaffolding necessary to encourage that kind of relationship building."

The grieving brain can render social-emotional competencies challenging to achieve because the downstairs brain and its resultant behaviors work biologically against the attainment of things like impulse control and emotional attunement. This can make caring relationships challenging to foster and maintain. But it's important to remember that, no matter the age of your students, every challenging behavior communicates a need. In this vein, students' disruptive behaviors are not bad—in fact, they're often reasonable, even inventive, strategies that help students meet their needs in challenging circumstances and situations. Although these behaviors can be disruptive, when we *recognize* and *respect* their usefulness and origins—the stories that underlie students' actions and reactions in the classroom—we can then *respond* by maintaining mindful awareness of the messages we send when interacting with students, ensuring that the impact of those cues aligns with our intent.

In Figure 3–1, you'll find example sentences that follow a three-part framework for responding to students' challenging grief behaviors: First, by *acknowledging and validating* students' emotional or behavioral states, we can meet them where they are and let them know they are seen and heard (so often, challenging behaviors come from the need to feel seen and heard). Next, we can *guide* students toward appropriate behavior by highlighting that, although their emotions are valid, their behavior is not helping to create an environment in which their or their peers' needs can be effectively met. Finally, we can use open-ended questions to *collaborate* with

1. "Tommy, I sense that you're feeling angry [sad, frustrated, other emotion word]. How can I best support you right now?"

2. "Xavier, I notice that you're not participating in class discussions as frequently as you used to, and I miss hearing your voice. What can we do to support you in sharing your ideas?"

3. "Marianna, I know that we're all having a lot of hard and confusing feelings right now. I certainly am. I want you to know that what you're feeling is OK, but it's not OK for you to express those feelings by hitting Tommy [calling out in class, telling Xavier to stop talking, etc.]. How about we practice some deep breathing for the next few minutes? I'll practice with you."

Note: Whenever possible, it's best to address student behavior after class time so as not to draw attention to and thereby reinforce interruptive actions with other students.

Figure 3–1   Sample Sentences for Responding to Challenging Grief Behaviors

students as we brainstorm effective ways to support their individual well-being and empower them to recognize the impact of their individual actions on other learners in the classroom.

Considering Culture

As teens' brains develop and they work to find and build the whole of their identities, so do their spiritual and cultural identities take a more defined shape. Teens' brains allow for increased abilities to think abstractly and analytically, meaning they gain the capacity to consider existential questions and to form their own opinions about—and actively choose to participate in—specific belief systems, rituals, and traditions (Nakkula and Toshalis 2006, 201). These processes necessarily involve considerations of mortality.

Western society is characteristically individualistic, avoidant when it comes to suffering and silent in the face of grief. Many non-Western cultures, on the other hand, normalize imagery and discourses about death and dying and take a communal approach to grieving and support. In *Culturally Responsive Teaching and the Brain*, Zaretta Hammond (2014) notes that cultural and familial norms similarly influence students' tendencies to gravitate toward individual or communal learning. She deems "high-trust, low-stress" (46) environments critical in culturally responsive education practices, which transfer to trauma- and grief-responsive approaches to creating safety in the classroom. In what ways do schools perpetuate Western perceptions of mortality? The texts we teach, the questions we ask during class discussions, and our own perceptions of students' expressions of loss influence, and are influenced by, our cultural identities and internalization of societal norms. How can we interrogate and leverage this self-understanding to support grieving students, to create "high-trust, low-stress" learning environments in which students feel safe to express who they are? Are we including non-Western perspectives (authors, creators, scientists, scholars) in our curricula? How do our cultural norms shape our relationships with grieving students, whether we identify with Western or non-Western culture?

By centralizing students' experiences—empowering them to speak up and out about their beliefs and realities through such strategies as open-ended questioning (more on this in Chapter 4), the Letters to a Listener activity (described later in this chapter), and the Milestone Memories activity (described later in this chapter), we can begin to cultivate environments and relationships in which a breadth of bereavement experiences are welcomed and supported.

Identity: A Conversation with Bridget Choo

Beyond the verbal and physical cues that contribute to affirming the experiences of grieving students, we can also conjure emotional safety through the affirmation of students' identities. In the breeze of a late summer day in 2019, I sat with Bridget Choo on her front porch. Bridget is an experienced independent school teacher, director of diversity, and past head of school. At the time of our conversation, she had started coursework for a PhD in language, literacy, and culture, with a research focus on the role of transitions in learning, motivated by the belief that "an invalidated identity really struggles to learn."

Bridget told me that, throughout her teaching career, she has discovered that grief and loss are critical transitions at play in every learning experience, "even teaching someone how to swim." She said:

> Those are experiences that everyone will go through, like sleep. Unfortunately, though, if there's not a space for [a] person to experience that fully, in a way that they need to, and not in the way that . . . Mom and Dad, or society, believes that they should, [it can do harm]. An individual needs to be in charge of how they process it, and I do believe that the adults—we create the safe space, and we allow that sort of freedom to explore, but I don't believe that everybody feels safe to begin with.

The idea that not every student "feels safe to begin with" connects heavily to matters of identity development and belonging at school, both of which are areas of Bridget's expertise. She defines emotional safety as "inviting identity into the classroom":

> From inviting family into the classroom . . . recognizing that learning happens outside of the classroom . . . inviting grand-parents, [whomever] that person deems as their family, because that may also be their friend group, maybe the neighbor, whoever they are. That creates a family feeling, or a community feeling of a group responsibility. Then, you take a look at how your classroom is physically set up. Do you have images on the wall that match that person's identity? And you don't have to have images on the wall, but if you choose to have images on the wall in contrast to who that person believes that they are, it is such a long shot for them to feel like they can get there. . . . Are they attainable images?

There is much research on identity representation in the classroom, as well as best practices for integrating social justice pedagogies across grade levels and subjects. Cory Collins (2019) writes in *Teaching Tolerance* magazine (now called *Learning for Justice*) about the ways in which teachers can unintentionally "erase" rather than "embrace" students' identities, especially by teaching through a lens of homogeneity (think: "I don't see color. You are my student, first.").

Claude Steele has exposed the ways in which "stereotype threat" places a psychological burden on students with marginalized identities, especially in contexts that traditionally exclude those facets of their selfhood—for example, female-identifying students in a math class (2011, 9). In the article "When Schools Cause Trauma," author Carrie Gaffney writes in conversation with Cornelius Minor, "For students who are struggling to build positive self-identity in the face of traumatizing, dehumanizing systems like racism or poverty, school should be a place where their identity is affirmed, not called into question" (2019). Such affirmation requires reciprocal expression—both verbal and nonverbal—between students, teachers, and community members, especially when loss or grief are impacting students' identity development. Bridget Choo elaborated:

> If a person feels the freedom to express themselves in a classroom, then they would feel safer to share the most sacred part of themselves, which is their pain—the most vulnerable part of themselves, which is their pain. Sometimes, people don't feel safe sharing even the most obvious parts of themselves—things that everybody can see and everybody knows. So, to create that place where somebody will share the parts that are still bleeding . . . [is] really about knowing your students, knowing who they are, asking them. . . . I also think dialogue journals are really important, where a student can have a private conversation with me whenever they need it.

You should never force grieving students to talk about their loss experiences (NASP School Safety and Crisis Response Committee 2015; Schonfeld and Quackenbush 2009, 46), but the act of telling stories—placing lived experiences within a narrative structure—can have incredible psychological, educational, developmental, and relational benefits. Because it's important to offer students opportunities for multimodal expression, as we know from our grief checklists in Chapter 2, inviting students to connect with one another as well as you, their teacher, through means other than dialogue (drawing, painting, writing) supports their grief literacy, or ability to articulate and understand their thoughts and feelings—an important practice outside of grief contexts, too.

The following activity, Letters to a Listener, is an adaptation of dialogue journals that allows teachers to implement and normalize the practice of multimodal communication at school.

Dialogue Journals: Letters to a Listener

OVERVIEW

Building upon the dialogue journals used by many teachers, Letters to a Listener is an interactive writing activity between students and teachers that facilitates multimodal communication. Because students who are experiencing difficult emotions may find it easier to write or draw about their thoughts and feelings than speak about them, this activity allows teachers to support healthy expression, social-emotional development, and relationship building with all students, including those who are grieving. Optional prompt-based writing can support students' emotional literacy and linguistic literacy simultaneously. Please note: the goal of this activity is not to force, or even ask, students to write about or articulate their grief, nor to position teachers as therapists, but rather to open and scaffold channels of communication between students and teachers that support the relationship building we know to be helpful in a grief context. Prompts are especially helpful for teachers who prefer more structured interaction.

Materials Needed
- journals, notebooks, or 8.5-by-11-inch paper
- pens, pencils, markers
- stickers or other decorations (for students to use in their notebooks)

Learning Objectives
Through participating in the Letters to a Listener activity, students will
- gain facility with expressive writing,
- strengthen metacognitive thinking and storytelling,

(continues)

- improve nonverbal social-emotional articulation,
- increase their ability to participate in intergenerational, interpersonal communication, and
- have a new tool with which to work through thoughts and feelings.

PROCEDURE

You may choose to design a physical mailbox for students' journals or set up regular times for journal collection with your students (biweekly, monthly). Let them know that you will write your response on the page following their last entry. If you and your students do not have access to journals or notebooks, creating stapled collections of writing on 8.5-by-11-inch paper works well, too.

Optional Scaffold

You may choose to share optional sentence starters or freewriting prompts with students who feel stuck. Things like "Tell me about a time when you felt strong" or "What makes you feel most proud?" offer positive frames for self-exploration. You can paste these prompts to the opening pages of students' journals, along with a statement about the journals' purpose, or offer provocations aloud on a day-by-day basis, perhaps aligned with curricular themes.

Problem-Solving

In the interest of transparency, you may consider sharing with students your role as a mandated reporter. Because students may disclose experiences with abuse (physical, emotional, sexual) or self-harm in their writing, you may prefer—depending on the age of your students—to make everyone aware that, although their letters are confidential, you will have to involve outside individuals should certain topics arise. Conversely, depending on your comfort level and the climate of your class, you may decide that such a forewarning would dissuade students' honesty, in which case you may decide to handle such disclosures on a case-by-case basis.

Example Teacher Narrative for Journaling

Here is how you can introduce this activity, without mentioning mandated reporting:

Today, I have a gift for you that I would like you to keep in your backpacks this year. I will pass around these journals, and you can pick whichever one you would like. Inside, please write your name and class year. We are going to use these to practice our letter writing skills.

Every week, I will set aside ten minutes for you to work on a letter, but you can write in your notebook anytime. You might choose to write to your future self, your current self, to me, or to a fictional or historical character. You might even write to someone different each time. I will collect your journals every two weeks and respond to your letters on the page following your last entry. I, too, will write in letter format so we can all enjoy receiving some snail mail. You might find this practice helpful when you need a brain break, or when you have a lot on your mind. Your journal is your space, and you shouldn't worry about spelling, grammar, or the quality of the writing. Follow your first thoughts, and allow your letters to unfold with them.

If you would like to mention mandated reporting, simply add the following:

The communications in these journals will be private between you and me. However, I want you to know ahead of time that I am required to share any writing that mentions harm being done to you, or harm that you have done to others, with school officials [you might give examples]. You can come to me with any topics of concern or write about them in this space, and I will keep your confidentiality in all possible instances.

Professional Support Extension

To maximize the critical ancillary support that a school psychologist, guidance counselor, or other administrative leader provides, adapt the Letters to a Listener program for a professional development context.

(continues)

(continued)

> If you are a counselor, create a mentor mailbox where
> teachers can submit anonymous letters, questions, or sce-
> narios regarding loss, trauma, or other social-emotional
> matters. Respond biweekly or monthly in a staff email
> or newsletter, offering advice and professional resources
> and inviting teachers to speak with you regarding their
> concerns. If you are a school leader, consider requiring
> every classroom teacher in your school to submit a letter
> to the mentor mailbox one or two times per year.

Elaborating on her prior comment about learning to swim, Bridget shared a story from her early teaching experiences in Thailand:

> I had a student . . . [who] was petrified of the water. He had
> watched his youngest sibling drown in the pool. He had some
> PTSD going on—full-body lockdown, trembling. But it was when
> we were able to really talk about it, and work with his peers,
> and share these stories about their youth, that he started to
> not feel so different about it. Just sharing their experience,
> even a little bit . . . you don't have to share everything, but if you
> start to share, or you start to hear other people's experiences,
> then you can take the next step, even if it's really small. I think
> that everyone needs to process their path on their terms. That
> enables them to take steps that we're not necessarily recog-
> nizing with our curriculum. But that curriculum will never go
> anywhere unless some of that happens.

It's important to remember, as I addressed in the introduction, that teachers are not trained therapists; they do not have the same interventional expertise, nor should they bear responsibility for the psychological challenges of grief and trauma. However, when symptoms of grief and trauma manifest organically in the learning environment, such as the scene that Bridget recounted, having a toolbox of responses, approaches, and even activities at hand to support all students' social-emotional wellness can alleviate both teacher and student and promote well-being for all. Sometimes, that well-being comes by way of storytelling, sharing pieces of ourselves in community. The following activity helps to scaffold such interaction.

Milestone Memories: A Time Line Activity

One way for students to share "even a little bit" is through the creation of "attainable images" showcasing their and their peers' lives. Milestone Memories is a time line activity in which students draw or depict and label defining moments in their lives. Sharing snippets of lived experience in the classroom frames and welcomes students' metacognitive thinking and identity development, two important components of grief-responsive teaching. Importantly, this activity does *not* require or even imply that students should share their experiences of grief or trauma but instead creates an opportunity for students to tell their peers and teachers who they are, on their own terms. For that reason, classwide sharing should always be optional.

Materials Needed

- paper or posterboard
- pencils, markers, pens
- optional: materials for collaging (magazines, photographs brought in by students, glue, scissors, etc.)
- optional: other decorative supplies as appropriate

Learning Objectives

By participating in this activity, students will:

- consider their identity and life experiences—what made them who they are today,
- identify and choose whether to share experiences that are important to them,
- build community by sharing on a challenge-by-choice basis, and
- practice storytelling in written, verbal, and visual formats.

(continues)

(continued)

PROCEDURE

1. Invite students to make a bulleted list of ten defining memories or moments in their lives. Where were they? Whom were they with? What were they doing, thinking, feeling, seeing?

2. What images or symbols best represent these experiences for students? Ask them to create one graphic representation (drawing, photograph, etc.) for each memory.

3. Determine the scale to which you'd like students to create their time lines. Invite them to label each memory and portray it with a corresponding image, either with markers and paper in class or on posters during a take-home assignment. With older students, you may use this activity as a provocation for further writing by encouraging students to create paragraph descriptions for each image or flash nonfiction scenes grounded in sensory details, concrete nouns, and other elements of storytelling.

4. Invite students to share their time lines with others via an optional gallery walk activity. Ask students to find two connections between their time line and those of others and two questions they have following their experience at the exhibition. What do they notice, and what do they wonder? How can you use these reflections to build community in your classroom and connect students to future assignments?

As a grief-responsive educator, you can relate theoretical information about identity development and belonging to emotional safety for bereaved students at school by considering how you make space for students' lived experiences in the classroom. Welcome and affirm grieving students' identities and stories; include bereaved characters, fictional or nonfictional, in narrative-based studies ("attainable images"); or implement activities that facilitate identity development or storytelling. Although grieving is an experience rather than an identity, loss is often born out of—and inevitably impacts—the systems that shape who we are. In an effort to honor the role that loss has in identity development, and the urgency that considerations of mortality can place upon that development, invite students to explore and express their evolving identities to the extent that feels comfortable for them. Such practices bolster interpersonal educational relationships—caring relationships—before and after a loss. They invite students to co-construct a safe space for themselves and their peers. And they allow the classroom to become "a well-lighted place." A house by a river. Accessible, humble, necessary.

Write and Reflect

Free-associate: What comes to mind when you hear the word *safety*? For five minutes, make a list; write bullet points or paragraphs; draw pictures or sketches representing what comes to mind. Consider when and where you've felt safety or a lack of it. Was this safety physical? Emotional? Relational? Write, draw, or sketch.

What Should I Say?

The Courage to Connect and Communicate with Grieving Students

Being unable to talk about my grief or loss . . . left me feeling depressed, confused, and terribly alone. A repressed conversation can occupy the same space in the psyche as a secret.

—MICHAEL HEBB, LET'S TALK ABOUT
  DEATH (OVER DINNER)

Every child deserves a champion—an adult who will never give up on them, who understands the power of connection and insists that they become the best that they can possibly be.

—RITA PIERSON, "EVERY KID NEEDS
  A CHAMPION"

I t was autumn, sunny, the last period of the day. High school hallways teemed with the excited chatter of teenagers, lockers clanging as students made their way out of a nearby class.

I sat on a blue plastic chair at the back of an English classroom as twenty or so students formed a circle with their desks. An aide whispered quietly to a student leafing through his folder, their dialogue a gentle hum against the backdrop of class discussion.

At the front of the room, the teacher transitioned from a discussion about literature to one about personal narrative writing. In preparation for their class together, she'd asked students to write a narrative essay exploring the themes of a recent read in relation to their life.

It was time to read their work aloud, their teacher told them, as many students averted her gaze. She made her way around the circle, calling each student by name.

From the mouths of these students unspooled stories examining family and work, dedication and resistance. In what ways does a tradesman and father in twenty-first-century America reflect Willy Loman from *Death of a Salesman*? In what ways does he differ?

Such were the kinds of questions examined implicitly in students' works.

When the teacher called upon one young man seated toward the back of the room, he read his narrative in a deep monotone, reciting as though his paper contained one long line. When he finished, he looked up, relieved and triumphant as he curled the sides of his printed paper with busied hands.

"And what are you leaving out?" his teacher asked.

"What do you mean?"

"You did not read your whole essay. Can you share with us what you left out?"

The boy reddened and retorted, "I'm not sure what you . . ."

"The part about your mom. You wrote about your mom."

"Oh, yeah . . . ," he said. "My mom has cancer."

It can feel intimidating to know how best to connect with bereaved students or any student facing adversity. It's as if grief is an umbrella that a student carries with them into class. They're under the shade of the umbrella, and there is no way for outsiders to truly know what the world looks like through its cover. Should we mention the umbrella, or should we pretend not to see it—treat them like every other student who doesn't have one? Should we compliment the umbrella? Question the umbrella? Demand that the student put the umbrella down? Or do we sit down next to the student, near their umbrella if not under it, and try to understand their experience carrying it? It must get uncomfortable, after all, holding its weight throughout the school day, with so many people like us wondering whether or not to address it.

The opening scenario represents a moment when, probably, everyone in the room felt uneasy. Western society, as a death-denialist culture, socializes us into freezing at mention of death, illness, and disability. We don't know what to say or when or how to say it. We don't want to make a mistake. We don't want to make things worse. We lean on platitudes: "Everything happens for a reason" or "Best wishes during this time." We tout positivity.

We feel unprepared to comfort the grieving and unheard when we are bereaved. We fear that we will say too much. That we have said too little. Sometimes, we say nothing at all. Other times, as in this scenario, our attempts at creating a classroom culture inclusive of students' experiences backfire.

This is a dance of stops and starts. Staccato.

A simple but powerful starting point for supporting grieving students comes from NPR education journalist Elissa Nadworny, who quotes Dr. David Schonfeld: "'Saying nothing says a lot, and that's a message we should never leave a child'" (2015).

There is a good chance that you are far more skilled at reaching out to and supporting students in times of tumult than you believe. Jana DeCristofaro, a licensed clinical social worker who is the community response coordinator at Dougy Center, the National Grief Center for Children and Families, recounted in our interview how teachers who have not yet had a bereaved student in class can employ the same strategies they use, consciously or subconsciously, with other students affected by trauma:

> It could be that students are experiencing these feelings [of grief] about any number of losses that aren't tied to death, and I wonder sometimes if that might help teachers feel a little bit more knowledgeable. . . . There are the people who

[have] a student [whose] dad died, and it's totally different than anything [they've] ever dealt with in [their] classroom before. Well, have you had a student who has dealt with going into the foster care system? Have you had a student who's dealt with a parent who has an ongoing addiction? Have you had a student in your classroom who has experienced any kind of trauma? I see a lot of the same things: difficulty concentrating, difficulty completing tasks, perhaps really big emotions that they're unable to modulate or mitigate in any way. Those were the things that we see in responding to trauma. You can utilize those skills and knowledge with kids who have had grief. Not to say that all grief is traumatic, but the [symptoms] are going to look very similar.

Taking the Plunge: Facilitating Supportive Conversations with Students

CODE, a four-step framework for having conversations with grieving students (see Figure 4–1), can guide you as you consider the best way to approach your students—to say something in a way that is both strategic and sincere, rooted in all that you know and can gauge regarding their particular situation, personality, and preferences. In short, conversations with grieving students should be *Compassionate*, *Open-ended*, *Direct*, and *Evolving*.

Reading the Tide: Navigating Vulnerability Through Responsive Strategies

It is important to note, in light of the vignette that opens this chapter, that supporting students through grief and adversity must begin on the relational level through one-on-one communication and support. We must take students' lead in regard to self-disclosure, and we should never put them on the spot or force their vulnerability.

Compassionate
Open-ended
Direct
Evolving

Compassionate

Approach students with empathy. Reflect on your own losses and the types of support that buoyed you in times of grief. It may seem obvious, but taking a compassionate, strengths-based approach to communications with grieving students by sharing genuine concern and respect for their realities is the most pivotal force undergirding healthy grief support at school. When you have one-on-one time with the impacted students, express concern in a private, gentle manner. Take their lead; honor their, as well as your own, boundaries; and follow your intuition.

Open-Ended

Rather than make assumptions or assertions about grieving students' realities, it is important for educators to open conversations with students using authentic, open-ended questions. Instead of statements like, "Let me know if you need anything," "You must be feeling sad," and "Your mom would be so proud of you," position students as the narrators of their experiences by asking open-ended questions, such as, "How can I help you right now?" or "How are you feeling?" or "How do you think your mom would feel about your accomplishments?" Asking students to tell you about the person whom they lost invites them to tell the story of their experience—a critical act in the grieving process—and affords you insight into the nature of their grief and how best to support them going forward (Coalition to Support Grieving Students n.d.).

Figure 4–1   CODE Framework

Direct

It's hard to talk about death. The sooner we can come to terms with that, the sooner we can conquer discomfort for the sake of our students and ourselves. Don't beat around the bush in conversations with bereaved students—or, worse, pretend that their loss never occurred. Feel comfortable mentioning their circumstances and opening doors to communication, even if they don't take you up on the opportunity at first. Never force students to talk about their grief, but know that consistent, clear messaging about your willingness to do so is an important part of relationship building in a grief context.

Evolving

As noted previously, grieving students may not feel comfortable opening up about their feelings or experiences. This is not a reflection of you but the reality that avoidance is a response to both grief and trauma. Because it is important not to push students' boundaries or meddle in deeply personal experiences, focus on the ways in which you can support students' overall well-being throughout the school year. Grief support is not limited to one attempt at discussion but extends to relationship building, social-emotional learning, and mentoring across time. Connect with students beyond curricula. Attend a sporting event. Share a favorite book. Emphasize a grieving student's growth in class, or compliment their resilience. Little by little, consistent, evolving acts of reaching out—whether about loss or not—build a relational foundation that is, in itself, an antidote to isolation and grief.

Throughout my work, I've come to identify three pitfalls in communicating with grieving students:

1. *Violated vulnerability*—A student offers a self-disclosure or confession that is somehow shared, publicized, judged or ridiculed, or otherwise used against the student.

2. *Forced vulnerability*—A student is put on the spot to self-disclose, publicly or privately. For example, a teacher says, "I'm not starting this tutoring session until you talk to me [open up to me, tell me about your feelings]." Self-disclosing assignments, such as personal narrative writing, may also fall into this category if we don't offer students choice or creative agency within the assignment structure.

3. *Ignored vulnerability*—A student moves toward self-disclosure or the sharing of emotions and the teacher brushes past, ignores, smooths over, or otherwise invalidates the articulation.

We can synthesize these three scenarios to find the correct calibration for connecting with bereaved students: *scaffolded vulnerability*. By opening opportunities for student-initiated communication, welcoming storytelling and articulations of identity in our classrooms, and directly addressing our willingness to think and talk about hard topics, we can build genuine relationships with students and support their gradual processing of lived experiences without risking further harm; we can create space for them to voice their realities—at whatever level feels comfortable to them—realizing that supportive relationships, whether or not they include direct discussions about grief, are most critical to combatting the potentially negative implications of grief and trauma. Effective social-emotional support is sometimes aided by, but not predicated on, teachers' or students' self-disclosure, so eliciting a discussion or confession should not be our goal so much as fostering an overall sense of connection tailored to the cues of individual students.

Research Shows Relationships Work

It takes only one person to ignite the powerful protective benefits of social connection in the lives of students dealing with trauma or loss (Bluestein 2001, 10). This means that you hold the power to change the trajectory of a grieving student's life, and your gestures of support need not be large: "If we can provide consistency, positivity, and integrity in all our interactions with our students, we'll establish a relationship that is safe enough for them," write trauma experts Kristen Souers and Pete Hall (2016, 80). From a smile to a kind comment (Bluestein 2001, 8), presence is paramount when seeking to become the professional, the person, the "champion" that educator Rita Pierson (2013) described in her TED talk. Laura Starecheski (2015) writes for NPR, "Having a grandparent who loves you, a teacher who understands and believes in you, or a trusted friend you can confide in may mitigate the long-term effects of early trauma." And medical researchers in *BMJ Open* affirm, "Interventions that enhance social support, or possibly perceptions of social support, may help reduce the burden of depression in older populations with ACE exposure" (Cheong et al. 2017, 1).

To dig more deeply into the power of sharing and listening in caring relationships, I spoke with Graham Bodie, PhD, professor of communication at the University of Mississippi and senior leader at the Listen First Project, a nonprofit coalition that cultivates respectful conversation across divides. Graham's research focuses on listening for social support, especially in times of bereavement.

> I'm reminded of Winnie the Pooh. [He] and Piglet are sitting on a log, and Piglet says, "I've had a bad day." Pooh says, "Do you want to talk about it?" and Piglet says, "No." So, he just sits there. And Piglet looks at him, like, "What are you doing?" He says, "Well, I'm just being with you." I think that's really powerful. But once [a person] starts talking, we are forced to make a decision. Do I talk? Do I remain silent? For some people, you absolutely do remain silent—no "aha," "yeah," or "right."

At the root of Graham's reflection is the truth that presence matters. Schonfeld's urging us to say something (Nadworny 2015) means, really, be there. Do not ignore what a grieving student is going through. Graham continued,

> In one sense, to be supportive means to embrace, or to hold, another person. I use [this] analogy: much like a column that supports the weight of the structure in a house or building, people start to support the weight of a stressful situation. Being supportive, both in the academic literatures, and just

anecdotally in your everyday experience, means to be there for someone, and in a lot of cases, the presence is enough.

Our presence or being there is enough—in fact, it's so strong—that there's a concept in psychology called "perceived support availability," which is the degree to which you believe that people in your social network will be supportive should you need to turn to them in times of stress. Research measures this as, not a personality characteristic necessarily, but acquainted to some sort of stable trait . . . some people have high degrees of perceived support availability while other people have a relatively low degree of perceived support availability, and it's related to attachment style. It's related to a lot of other kinds of traits, facets of individual differences.

Graham summarized his research by sharing the following directives: "Sit with somebody who's had a bad day. Let them know you care. Be there for them, should they eventually want to talk about it." In Chapter 2, I talked about the ways in which relationships are built as strata, how—layer by layer—we come to know our students, and they in turn come to know us. We study each other's preferences, quirks, comfort zones, and communication styles. We often begin with low-risk topics and ascend to matters of the heart and mind.

We can leverage these relationships for the purposes of grief support by communicating laterally with young people. Picture Pooh sitting by Piglet's side. Imagine sitting next to the grief umbrella. Rather than forcing or ignoring conversations about grief, consider how to build and then utilize your relationship with a grieving student, even—and perhaps especially—outside of a grief context, to support their development.

The Role of Story in Support

Here's a striking story about perceived support availability and the power of feeling seen and heard: One day, when Bluestein was conducting research for her book on emotional safety in schools, she sat amid a bustling kindergarten classroom and noticed a student whispering to the wall (2001, 235). After inquiring of the teacher, Bluestein became acquainted with Mrs. Murphy—a drawing of an elderly woman tacked to the bulletin board for those times when a student had a story to share, but their teacher was busy helping someone else.

The technique was not unique, nor limited to the younger grades, Bluestein later learned: in an interview with a seventh-grade teacher, she was introduced to a "talk to the ear" system—the teacher had taped a large paper ear to the door of the classroom. "This need for connection is particularly strong for kids in crisis," she writes (236). Middle schoolers took to the practice as faithfully as their younger peers.

Is this an effective way to manage students' emotional lives? What if the students who are talking to their ear, or their Mrs. Murphy, have legitimately important conflicts or concerns to discuss? What if they neglect to follow up with their teacher after sharing with Mrs. Murphy? What if a consequential self-disclosure is overlooked? Is this approach supportive or dismissive?

When thinking about adolescent students, this "need for connection . . . in crisis" offers a new frame through which to view social media. Are the likes and comments elicited by a grief-related post truly supportive or perceived to be? What does a student garner out of technological grieving? "Grief within the context of shared trauma and violence is a collective experience," researchers wrote (Patton et al. 2018, 7), reflecting on a cohort of grieving, gang-involved teens who turned to Twitter to express their loss. "We advance this argument by offering Twitter as a new context where expressions of grief have a social meaning" (7).

We are meaning-making creatures, and we make meaning of our lives through storytelling (Cron 2012, 19; Haven 2007, 104). A narrative structure requires us to align our experiences within a story arc, and doing so helps us condense and process what can otherwise seem incomprehensible. Stories have resolution, or at least a culminating revelation. We, too, must reach a level of resolution or revelation when we pour our grief into story structure, even if that story structure is imposed by a subconscious author.

When we listen to stories, our brains produce oxytocin—"the moral molecule" (Zak 2012, 24)—a critical neurotransmitter in empathy and attachment. Our brains need stories to foster and sustain connection, and our hearts need connection during hardship. "The need to share is an essential urge within the grieving process," add Kakar and Oberoi. "Research suggests that sharing is helpful as part of the search for meaning, allowing individuals the opportunity to make sense of the loss (Tyma, 2008). Meaning making remains a critical component of the grieving process and it appears that . . . members are able to adopt a macro perspective, beginning the process of meaning making (Castle and Phillips, 2003)" (Kakar and Oberoi 2016, 374).

Mining these stories—Mrs. Murphy, the ear, Twitter—we can extract a critical act in grief support: bearing witness, holding space, and making room for articulation, verbal or nonverbal. We can realize that listening—receiving and validating a student's story—is often more important than talking. And this may assuage the anxiety most of us feel when grappling for language in the face of loss. Our being available, clearly and consistently, and trying our best to keep our own grief hang-ups (fear of death, painful reminders of our own grief, fear of messing up) from getting in the way of a student's emotional work, is enough to ignite healing and combat the negative impacts of grief and trauma in students' lives.

We began this chapter by learning that it takes only one person to buoy a student in times of hardship. Leading trauma researcher Bessel van der Kolk confirms, "Knowing that we are seen and heard by the important people in our lives can make us feel calm and safe. . . . Focused attunement with another person can shift us out of disorganized and fearful states" (2014, 80). Acts of sharing and storytelling, when met with a safe and supportive witness, allow one's public story and inner experience to begin to meld as the sharer gains practice in naming the events that have shaped their lives, and the emotions elicited by them.

Ten years after I sat in front of many caring teachers as my bunched-up, sophomore self, I wish that I could sit down next to my own grief umbrella. I would place a hand on that girl's shoulder and invite her take a deep breath. I would tell her that, although it is hard, with a trusted and trusting listener, talking helps; talking heals. Through talking, we peek out from the shade of our stories to discover that others carry umbrellas, too. And those umbrellas do not make us weird or different but strong, insightful, and attuned— if we let them.

Communities of Connection

Psychologist Urie Bronfenbrenner established the Bioecological Systems Theory of Development to explore the constellation of communities with which people interact, all of which have varying influences on that person's identity and social-emotional selfhood. Like matryoshka dolls, the five systems are situated within one another (see Figure 4–2), interconnected yet separate, with varying potencies and impacts. Importantly, developmental psychologists have expanded and built upon this framework to create models that are more culturally relevant. The original framework includes the following systems (Nakkula and Toshalis 2006, 249; Guy-Evans 2020):

1. *The individual*, who has specified traits: sex, age, health status, and so on.

2. *The microsystem*—one's closest relations: immediate family members, close friends, the people with whom one lives.

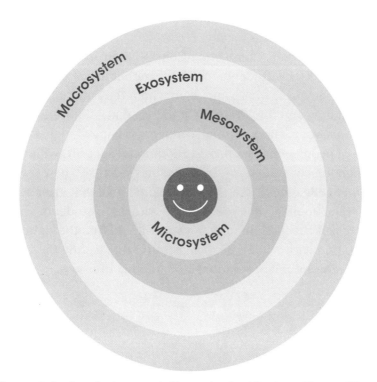

Figure 4-2   Bronfenbrenner's Bioecological Systems Theory Diagram

3. *The mesosystem*—one's school, neighborhood, places of work and worship. (There may be some fluidity between the mesosystem and the microsystem; for example, key individuals at school could fall within the microsystem for some students, while household family members could move into the mesosystem. Physical proximity does not necessarily indicate social or emotional closeness.)

4. *The exosystem*—external influences such as news, media, a parent's or partner's workplace (a bad day at work can influence a person's behavior at home, thereby impacting the microsystem).

5. *The macrosystem*—societal and cultural standards, norms, values, and laws.

Grief has the potential to upend relationality as we know it. Depending on the system in which a loss occurs, its proximity to the individual, and the ways in which it rearranges the constellatory system pictured, its impact can alter one's entire bioecological sphere. This means that grief support can also happen at, and ripple throughout, multiple levels.

The following activity, Connection Constellation, offers an entry point for you and your students to think together about the systems within which they live; where and from whom they might garner support; and how and for whom their actions make a difference.

For your and your students' sake, connect grieving students with a network of people who can provide additional support. Widen their connection constellations. Introducing students to new peers, coaches, and colleagues lessens the emotional load that grief support can have when you feel that you are sole witness to students' stress. It also increases the likelihood that a student will find the right match, a person with whom they feel comfortable testing the waters of personal storytelling or relationship building after loss.

Connection Constellation Inspired by Bronfenbrenner's Bioecological Systems Theory

In this activity, students will reflect upon, critically examine, and create visual representations of the varying levels of support and relationships in their lives as well as the ways in which those networks influence their individual identity.

Materials Needed

- 8.5-by-11-inch notebook or construction paper
- pens, pencils, markers
- optional: string, yarn, or twine (to connect relationship dots)

Learning Objectives

Upon completing this activity, students will

- gain knowledge and awareness of the people, communities, and resources that they can turn to for support in times of challenge,
- understand and articulate some of the relational factors influencing their identities, and
- understand and articulate the reciprocal nature of relationships and the ways in which they as individuals are not only connected to but also influence their constellation.

PROCEDURE

1. Pass around notebook paper or construction paper, markers, pens, and other drawing utensils.

2. Ask each student to make a list of ten important people or influences in their life and write the names of those people, places, or things on the back of their paper. If students have difficulty brainstorming ten people or influences, push them to consider those individuals who play important roles

(continues)

(continued)

in their life but may not be readily obvious (How about a postal person? A neighbor? A favorite singer or author or athlete?). They can include people who are no longer living.

3. On the front of their paper, invite students to draw ten dots, one per important person or influence.

4. Invite students to draw an eleventh dot. This dot represents themselves.

5. Beneath each dot, have students list the name of the person, place, or thing that it represents.

6. Once they have labeled all dots, invite students to connect the dots by drawing lines between them in whatever design they wish. This will be their connection constellation.

7. Ask students to name their constellation and write its name at the top of the paper.

8. Encourage students to hold onto these drawings for times when they might be feeling lonely or frightened. Share with them that these constellations are visual reminders of the people and influences that are important to them and to whom they are important, too. The drawings, like students' brain building drawings from Chapter 1, provide blueprints for reaching out and seeking connection in times of hardship.

Teacher Narrative

Let's go around and share our favorite constellations. Share their names and tell us what you like about them or what you have noticed. *[Group shares.]*

Today, we are going to think about how the different communities in our lives form their own constellations. Who knows what *identity* means? What is our identity, and what is it made up of? *[Group shares; teacher records thoughts on the board.]*

A scientist named Urie Bronfenbrenner was fascinated by this question. He wanted to understand more about how the different communities we live and grow in impact who we are and who we become. He created a theory that named five different types of communities we all take part in. Let's take a look at them together. *[Draw or display Bronfenbrenner's concentric circle diagram (Figure 4–2) on the board, labeling each ring and sharing with students whom these rings represent; with older students you can introduce the terms micro-, meso-, exo-, and macrosystem; with younger students— for example, those in fifth or sixth grade—you might instead number each ring from one to five, with one being the closest (individual).]*

Today, we are going to make our own identity constellations, taking into consideration Bronfenbrenner's theory. Think about the different systems in your life—the different people, places, and communities that impact you and that you impact. Write a list of ten important people or influences in your life (for example, a pet, a favorite place in nature, a community or faith-based organization, an activity).

Optional Extension

For a visual display of interconnectedness, give students the option to hang their connection constellations on a bulletin board. Remind them that your classroom is also a constellation, that every student and teacher in the room (and school) is connected. All of the individual constellations therefore conjoin into one larger constellation or solar system. You might choose to take yarn or twine and connect students' drawings in a large spider web pattern, attaching the twine to the tape or tack of each picture. Share with students, again, the metaphorical significance, asking them to look at the dot that represents themselves, reiterating how the constellation would not be the same if their dot weren't in its place, reminding them of their unique individuality and the community in which they exist. Tie this demonstration back to Bronfenbrenner's model.

(continues)

(continued)

Professional Development Extension

Make your own Connection Constellation alongside students to emphasize that social support is important at any age. Consider implementing the exercise with colleagues during discussions about compassion fatigue and secondary traumatic stress (see Chapter 8), to solidify whom and what in your respective circles you can turn to when refueling.

Roger's Story

Roger loved taking risks. He had a rebellious streak. However, at thirteen years old, when his mother was diagnosed with small-cell lung cancer and given less than twelve months to live, Roger knew that he had to temper those tendencies to reduce the amount of stress that he placed on his family. This is the story that he shared as a guest on the *Trauma Talks* podcast, sponsored by the University at Buffalo's Institute on Trauma and Trauma-Informed Care.

Five and a half months passed between Roger's mom's diagnosis and her death, after which, listeners learned, risk offered Roger not only a rush but an escape. "I fell into a long stream of drug abuse and self-destruction, essentially," he shared (Institute on Trauma and Trauma-Informed Care 2016), recounting that—after his loss—he stopped playing sports and resigned from the community groups and extracurriculars he once actively participated in. "When I was sixteen, after seeing the guidance counselor at my high school fairly frequently, I ended up being persuaded after a number of months to speak to a counselor one on one about the death of my mom and my maladaptive coping strategies I'd developed since then."

In his podcast episode, Roger went on to describe that, in addition to addiction and feelings of apathy, grief changed his behavior in the ways we explored in previous chapters: suddenly, he found himself fighting with classmates, disrespecting teachers, and acting up at school. "One of my idols that I still talk to and respect to this day, a teacher at the school, took me aside after class one day and told me that, if I didn't go speak to a counselor, that she was going to call them," Roger shared, reflecting on a turning point in his development. "I decided to take her advice or her persuasion there, and I went to see a Nexis youth group counselor in my home town near Toronto."

Today, Roger is a peer counselor to other young people struggling in the ways that he did following the death of his mom. He cited the "empowering pressure" that mentors in his life ("a few teachers, the guidance counselor, the principal, the chaplain") placed upon him as a pivotal force in helping him navigate that "dark point." His mentors introduced him to two practices that continue to offer him reprieve: journaling and yoga.

Roger's story is a powerful example of the ways in which a team of supporters can alter the trajectory of a grieving student's life. "None of us are immune from life's tragic moments," writes retired Navy admiral William H. McRaven in his graduation-speech-turned-book *Make Your Bed*. "Like the small rubber boat we had in basic SEAL training, it takes a team of good people to get you to your destination in life. You cannot paddle the boat alone" (2017, 21). Jana, the community response coordinator at Dougy Center, whom we heard from earlier in this chapter, reminds teachers that they do not have to be *that* person—the supporter, the encourager, the listener—for every student. There are people for whom, and times in which, you may not be emotionally available. You may not be able to support all of the Rogers who walk through your door, and that is OK. Jana says teachers must "recogniz[e] that not every teacher has to be the same level of support for every student." To McRaven's point, "a team of good people" can distribute the onus of support in times of student need. Jana elaborates:

> I think about one teen who came to the Dougy Center, and there was one teacher they felt really close and connected to. They were in high school. If they needed to take a break, there was an agreement with the other teachers that they could take a break and go to that teacher's classroom if they weren't in that class. Maybe that student has ten teachers— they only needed one whom they could count on. So, those

other nine just had to have the flexibility and the awareness to create that or remember that that student could access that relationship. Not every teacher has to be the perfect support . . . they [just] maybe [need to] not stand in the way of [a student] getting the support that they know they need.

Consider yourself one critical piece in the puzzle of grief support and one corner in your classroom constellation. Your words matter. Your actions matter. Your silences matter. Think about the kind of difference that you would like to make.

Know that you can.

A Note About Therapy Referrals

It's important, when supporting grieving students, to utilize and facilitate connections between outside resources and professionals whose specialized training transcends your own. School counselors, grief groups, and external therapists or psychiatrists may all play a role in the effective support of someone who is grieving. Certainly, if you perceive that a student is a potential threat to themselves or others, true to your responsibility as a mandated reporter, you must seek help from professionals right away. However, in the case of caring relationships with students whose situations seem tragic but less urgent, be mindful of how and when you introduce and frame the act of help seeking. For example, if a student opens up about difficult emotions, and you ask, "Do you see someone to talk about this?" this well-intentioned comment of concern could be perceived as dismissive or judgmental, further silencing a student who may just be starting to speak about their loss, implying that they should not open up to you or are wrong to articulate their experiences.

Because we know from Chapter 1 that grief is natural, healthy, and in most cases nonpathological, we must normalize students' articulations of grief without reflexively implying that the topic does not belong in our relationships.

Then, in the context of a caring relationship, we can work to normalize and destigmatize acts of help seeking and conversations around mental health gradually, posing therapy as an additional, helpful option available to everyone, no matter what they are going through. Speaking from the "I" perspective can be helpful here, when executed strategically. Saying something like, "I attended a grief group after the loss of my sister and it really helped me to feel heard," is one way to connect laterally with grieving students without divulging too much personal information.

Write and Reflect

What might you say to a grieving student when you approach them? Based on what you've learned in this chapter, jot down some sentence starters using the CODE guide as inspiration. Practice these sentence starters to have them handy in times of need.

How Can I Teach and Talk About Loss in Class?

Navigating Grief and Mortality in Curricula

That was the rule that you never mixed up troubles at home with life at school. When parents were poor or ignorant or mean, or even just didn't believe in having a TV set, it was up to their kids to protect them.

—KATHERINE PATERSON, BRIDGE TO TERABITHIA

Without a Thou, there is no I evolving. Without an It there is no context, no figure and no heat, but only an affair of mirrors confronting each other.

—DAVID HAWKINS, THE INFORMED VISION: ESSAYS ON LEARNING AND HUMAN NATURE

**"W**hen you're afraid, you can't do very much learning," Glenn Manning told me as he recounted teaching high school English after a number of student suicides took place in his district.

The [tragedies] changed not only the texts that we considered teaching but also the ways that we considered teaching them. There was ongoing conversation about the extent to which we should protect young people from difficult texts or the extent to which we should expose them, with the right support, to difficult texts. And maybe even some folks were thinking that we should continue on as usual—their thinking was that we should prepare the child for the path, not the path for the child. I was in the camp that said, "It's important that we help young folks who become faced with difficulty, an obstacle, but we don't need to expose them to one [unnecessarily]."

As an example, [in my English class] I had the brother of one of the students who took [their] own life. We were reading *Catcher in the Rye*, and in that text there's a tertiary character that you don't learn much about other than the fact that they jumped out of the window. So, I did have to approach that really carefully, and it was apparent that this person's parents, on school night, had a lot of hard questions about why we were teaching this text. I had to say to them that we are unfortunately not able to absolutely avoid difficult topics. Literature is driven by conflict; it's what drives a story forward. But it was really important for me in that moment to listen as opposed to talk and to hear what the parent was saying and try to empathize with them while, at the same time, respond in a way that put them hopefully at ease about the level of support that their son was going to get from me—how we would read this work, and what it [might] mean to him, and that [reading and writing can be] a way of working through and processing some of the grief that [one] may feel. . . . It encourages a level of introspection, reflection, on the part of the practitioner—the teacher.

From a sixth-grade study of *Bridge to Terabithia* to a senior history class analyzing *Night* by Elie Weisel, from journalism students at Marjorie Stoneman Douglas chronicling the wake of a school shooting for their school newspaper to a science class studying the life cycle, the theme of mortality is inevitable across curricula, and the questions that Glenn raises regarding protection and exposure reveal the underbelly of a tension all teachers must eventually face: when we are confronted with mortality by way of classroom content or current events, what is the correct calibration for confronting the topic in our classroom discourse and curricula? Should we seize the opportunity to explore this theme explicitly, or might that be too much for our students (and, perhaps, ourselves)? Do we brush past the theme entirely and focus on the many other topics available to us—the complexities of aging and epigenetics in the life cycle, for example, or the use of figurative language in a text? Should we skirt around mortality? Address it abstractly or directly? What if we know someone in our classroom is actively grieving—what then?

"The truth lies somewhere in the middle," my father was known to say, and it seems pertinent to invoke that idiom here: teachers are the experts on their students' specific needs, their classroom culture, and the extent to which they feel comfortable addressing and opening space for considerations of mortality in curricula. This chapter seeks not to offer concrete directives, realizing the subjective and situational nature of this sensitive topic, but to instead offer insight into the pros, cons, and options available to you as "the practitioner—the teacher."

Content Warnings, Challenge by Choice, and Personal-Care Permission Slips

Content warnings are a controversial topic in educational discourses surrounding work with teens. (Note: In line with recent evidence regarding the problematic terminology of *trigger warnings*, I employ the terms *content warnings* and *grief reminders* instead.) As Glenn noted, teachers, parents, and students diverge when considering whether to prepare "the child for the path" or "the path for the child."

Scientific studies have yielded shaky results regarding the efficacy of content warnings (Dolan 2018); however, literature regarding grief and bereavement suggest that their use is worthwhile, especially when paired with other grief-responsive teaching strategies.

The words of Nadworny, Schonfeld, and others cited throughout this book implore teachers not to "turn to avoidance," true to the "say something" edict, realizing that silence can perpetuate social and psychological harm. It makes sense that relational entities like empathy and executive functioning require the acceptance and synthesis of emotion, rather than an avoidance of it. But because the grieving process is not linear and often naturally involves an adaptive avoidance on the part of both adults and adolescents, we can again find guidance in a both-and versus an either-or approach when monitoring and sharing curricular materials that may provoke challenging emotions or memories for students in our classrooms.

In a professional development resource titled "Grief Triggers," the Coalition to Support Grieving Students (n.d.) states, "Grief triggers are sudden reminders of the person who died that cause powerful emotional responses in grieving children. They are most common in the first few months after the death, but may happen at any time." Such reminders are often unexpected and unavoidable:

> In a school setting, the class may be talking about a city in social studies that reminds the student of a prior family vacation and special time spent with the deceased. A peer may comment over lunch about a television show the student had always watched with a sibling who died. The class may be asked to discuss an assignment with their mother or father, and the student is reminded that she no longer has two parents. Almost anything can serve as a grief trigger. (Coalition to Support Grieving Students n.d.)

There is no way for teachers to be made privy to all possible reminders of grief for their students. Teachers may not even be aware of who in their classroom is actively grieving. Because of these gaps in knowledge, instituting broad-brush support for all students and differentiating with those students who you know to be at higher risk or actively processing grief or trauma creates a classroom culture that catalyzes learning and growth.

Anticipating and assuaging grief reminders by using content warnings when curricular content addresses death, violence, abuse, or suicide allows teachers to not protect students from the harsh realities of the world, as some critics may say, but prepare them for potential threats to a level of well-being they may be working hard to maintain.

Another strategy that the Coalition to Support Grieving Students suggests is to collaborate with students to create a plan for those times when grief reminders may interrupt their learning. My iteration of this technique involves creating personal-care permission slips for yourself and your students, which you might introduce and assign at the start of the year while establishing classroom norms or at the beginning of a unit that you know to be especially challenging, like a study of Holocaust literature. Create a personal-care permission slip alongside your students to level the hierarchical playing field, humanizing and acknowledging the reality that both teachers and students are vulnerable to loss and can practice self-care in the face of it.

Personal-Care Permission Slips

OVERVIEW

This activity will encourage students to think proactively and self-reflectively about regulatory behaviors that they can practice if or when they feel dysregulated in the classroom environment. Teachers should create these slips alongside their students to normalize conversations about self-care across age ranges. The activity melds nicely with beginning-of-year discussions about classroom culture, expectations, and norms, but you can implement the practice at any time and regularly refer back to students' slips throughout the year.

Materials Needed

1. 8.5-by-11-inch paper
2. pens, pencils, markers
3. other decorative supplies

Learning Objectives

Through creating Personal-Care Permission Slips, students will:
- practice self-reflection,
- identify how emotional regulation and dysregulation manifest in their bodies and behaviors,

- make connections between feelings, behaviors, and needs,
- learn to articulate, self-advocate, and proactively plan for identified needs, and
- practice self-care and build community by enacting their plans as needed.

PROCEDURE

Invite students to decorate their permission slips however they wish and respond to the following prompts:

Permission Slip

I, _____, hereby declare the right and responsibility to recognize and attend to my well-being.

When I'm feeling, _____, or _____. I can count on _____ to help me talk through my feelings.

During the school day, strategies I can turn to include _____, _____, and _____.

In class, I can _____.

After class, I can talk to _____ or engage in _____ to help clear my mind.

Things my teacher can do to help me during these moments include

_____

_____

_____

Student Signature: _____

Teacher Signature: _____

(continues)

(continued)

Once students have completed their slips, ask them to keep a copy handy throughout the year—in a folder, backpack, or binder. You might also choose to scan copies of the slips into a digital file in case students misplace their copies throughout the year. Invite students to adapt or revise these slips as necessary, should their needs—or their thinking about their needs—change across time.

Another easy-to-use activity, the Well-Being Barometer, offers an efficient way to gauge students' responses to content and normalize the verbalization and sharing of emotional states—a necessary precursor to executive functioning and personal care. In my conversation with Priscilla Kane Hellweg, educator and executive director of Enchanted Circle Theater, she shared, "We learn to read the room. As a teacher, you're constantly reading the room and seeing where people are at, and who's with you, who's not, [and] where they are when they're not with [you]. [We] have to process and make those sorts of immediate decisions, and it's always a reminder that everybody has gone through stuff, and is going through stuff, and to stay open and present."

The following activity makes visible your "reading of the room" and invites students to join in.

Well-Being Barometer: Reading the Room

OVERVIEW

Priscilla notes the importance of "reading the room" in a trauma or grief context. Teachers do this all of the time, scanning the emotional, physical, attentional, and attitudinal climate throughout each class period and adjusting their engagement strategies accordingly.

This activity offers a visual way for teachers and students to gauge the state of the room together, calling social-emotional well-being to students' minds, encouraging them to check in with themselves, and offering a tool for teachers to use when gauging the efficacy of interventional exercises like mindfulness practices or to touch base about the impact of potentially challenging curricular content.

Materials Needed

- optional: laminated yellow, green, and red circles that students can use as stoplights to represent their emotional states (this is especially applicable in younger grades)

Learning Objectives

By participating in this activity, students will:

- practice noticing their social-emotional states throughout the school day,
- attune to the impacts of external and internal factors that impact their social-emotional well-being,
- inform teachers' instructional decisions through nonverbal articulation of their social-emotional states,
- increase self-awareness and metacognitive thinking skills, and
- consider how emotional awareness can promote regulation.

PROCEDURE

At the beginning of class, ask each student to share their "traffic light feelings" verbally or by drawing a circle on a piece of paper and labeling it "red," "yellow," or "green." You might share traffic light cards with students, one for each color, and ask that they store them in their desks throughout the year. Pair each color with feeling words: Red, for example, might mean *tired, sad, mad, bored*; yellow, *just OK*; and green, *good, energized, happy, ready to learn.*

With older students, you may request a visual display, such as "thumbs up, down, or half and half," or a numerical display of one to five fingers, where one means *tired, sad, mad,* or *bored* and five means *great.*

In this exercise, don't ask for, or allow explanations for, students' ratings. Instead, use these tools to understand the state of your classroom en masse. For students whose ratings are low, make a mental note to follow up with a check-in after the lesson.

(continues)

(continued)

Adaptation

You might use "reading the room" exercises as introductory and exit activities to gauge the emotional impact of a lesson on students. For example, when implementing classroom activities grounded in mindfulness practices—as discussed later in this book—asking for students' traffic light feelings affords them (and you) a barometer for measuring the efficacy of intervention techniques. Additionally, gauging the emotional climate before and after a lesson that required a content warning gives further insight into the emotional exertion that the lesson demanded and whether it makes sense to remind students of their personal-care permission slips.

Educators may enact any of these strategies in anticipation of grief reminders—again, not out of avoidance on the part of teacher or student, but in recognition of the diverse ways in which grieving students come to grapple with their emotions and lived experiences and out of a desire to empower those students to exert agency in their learning and prioritize their personal needs. Nearly every teacher and grief expert interviewed for this text noted that content warnings were integral in their shaping a safe space for young people. They employed content warnings to create a culture in which direct considerations of mortality could take place; rather than perpetuate avoidance, the warnings allowed group members to sidle up to the topic at whatever distance felt safe to them. If we are to consider curricula as a potential catalyst for understanding mortality, and use that understanding to propel learning and growth, we must first lay the foundation for students' self-advocacy and safety or else risk perpetuating trauma.

Taking a challenge-by-choice approach in your classroom by offering students alternative texts or assignments; creating, referencing, and updating personal-care plans; and employing content warnings allows you to be proactive, recognizing that—regardless of the ease with which a student perceivably copes with and adjusts to loss—bereavement rearranges one's mind, body, and surroundings—the curve and terrain of "the path"—impeding or empowering learning along the way, depending on how we respond to it.

Developmental Depth: How Teens' Brains Facilitate New Frames for Learning

Glenn touches on the notion that exploring mortality through literature catalyzes students' introspection, metacognition, and overall thinking and feeling, in a way that can lead to healing and growth. His observations are especially pertinent in a developmental context. As adolescents acquire increased abilities to think abstractly and engage in perspective taking, so do they experience shifts in their understandings of mortality and grief, whether their own or others', which might be reflected in their engagement with curricula. For example, as teens gain the ability to grapple with textual analysis and meta-meaning with enhanced nuance, so are they able to advance from concrete, binary understandings of life and death to abstract existential questions surrounding loss, love, belief, and causality—themes that undergird all we think and do as adults and that often permeate the texts, films, or other content that we study together in classrooms.

These deepened understandings may not translate into adolescents' behaviors and self-perceptions. For example, no matter their increased understanding of mortality, teens' brains will continue to make them feel immortal, not yet inhibiting risk-taking behaviors that would make a mortality-aware adult shake their head. However, they do open a new range of thoughts, questions, and emotions, expanding and complexifying opportunities for curricular engagement and discussion in class. We'll now explore a few frameworks that you might use to structure such discussions with your students.

Curricular Catalysts: Exploring Relationships Between Texts, Self, and World

"Who am I?" is the question at the core of adolescence; identity development is the task set before teens as they prepare to enter an increasingly complex world. The question is all consuming as teens try out and negotiate new and different roles, exercise increased independence, peer dependence, and self-awareness on their journey toward claiming an individual identity. The question is even more consuming in the context of life after loss. In a classroom setting, we can leverage this developmental question to spur intrinsic motivation through two educational frameworks, the first a philosophy, the second a strategy.

1. *I, Thou, and It* (Hawkins Centers of Learning n.d.):

> Watch yourself when you meet a new person—it is when you find some common ground that the relationship becomes interesting. Watch two children negotiate during play—how easily a conflict can be resolved when the end goal is to continue a mutually interesting game. When two human beings share a mutual interest, the spark and excitement surrounding exploring this interest is electrifying. (Hawkins Center of Learning n.d.)

Originally designed to describe powerful learning moments in science and math curricula, the I, Thou, and It framework explores the relational and intellectual synergy—the "three-way relationship"—at play when both students and teachers learn reciprocally from one another as co-observers and co-investigators in the pursuit of original inquiry. Rather than pose teachers as experts who impart wisdom unto children through a transaction of knowledge, this framework posits that powerful learning must involve unanswered (and even unanswerable) curiosities that students and teachers pursue together, as collaborators, connecting with one another while relating new knowledge to lived experiences, acknowledging commonalities, and learning from differences.

2. *Text-to-Text, Text-to-Self, Text-to-World* (Facing History and Ourselves 2021): This teaching strategy invites students to relate a text (book, film, artwork, etc.) to another text; to themselves; and to local or global communities through considerations of history, science, current events, and so on. Worksheets with inquiry-based provocations are available at https://www.facinghistory.org.

If we assume that a student is always asking, implicitly, "Who am I?" (and, as they age, perhaps, "Who are we?," in regard to identity- and community-based belonging), how might that change the texts that we teach; the ways we communicate relevance; the range of identities we present to students by way of literature; the strategies we use to facilitate and eke out those connections between self, other, and world?

Is our content representative? And what does this mean in relation to the theme of loss?

In a grief context, the two strategies allow teachers to structure considerations of mortality using mentor texts as vehicles for self-exploration, relational learning, and content acquisition. Loss changes and challenges the question "Who am I?" and literature, no matter the discipline, offers a mirror and a window (Style 1988). When teachers like Glenn grapple with how to teach a text involving death or grief, they humanize the issue—the *it*—by approaching content as a co-learner: Invite students to consider the theme of mortality alongside you by exploring an array of texts, creating opportunities for them to share their lived experiences through storytelling and make connections between literature and their local and global communities. Perhaps Sally's great aunt is a Holocaust survivor whose stories impact Sally's reading of *Night* or *The Diary of Anne Frank*. Or maybe Noah, whose brother died in Afghanistan, brings to his study of *The Things They Carried* a nuanced understanding of honor and sacrifice.

Loss can be a catalyst for learning. By making connections between the texts we study, the people we are, and the communities we inhabit, we facilitate the integration of students' minds and hearts. We leverage personal relevance to push students' thinking beyond the familiar. We empower students to utilize their expertise in the classroom. And we collaboratively consider the implications of loss in literature and life. Here are two writing prompts that encourage students to make text-self-world connections through personal narrative and analytical writing:

Personal Narrative Prompt Example

Both Shakespeare's *Hamlet* and Angie Thomas' *The Hate U Give* engage themes of adversity, loss, resilience, and the search for meaning. Though the texts seem quite different, consider the commonalities between lines such as "I can't change where I come from or what I've been through, so why should I be ashamed of what makes me, me?" (Thomas 2017, 441) and "This above all: to thine own self be true"

(Shakespeare 1992, 42). In a personal narrative essay, practice using concrete nouns, sensory descriptions, and dialogue to create scenes relating a moment from your life to the themes of these texts. When have you, like Hamlet or Starr, confronted life, love, or loss and found deeper meaning? In what ways have you stayed true to yourself even when the act took courage in the face of challenge? At the end of your piece, include an author's note explaining how these texts relate to your narrative.

Literary Analysis Prompt Example

In Shakespeare's *Hamlet* and Angie Thomas' *The Hate U Give*, the protagonists grapple with grief over lost friends and loved ones. In an analytical essay, compare and contrast these seemingly different texts considering the theme of mortality and the role of context. How do characters' identities (race, class, gender, time period) influence their losses? What literary techniques (dialogue, figurative language, sensory imagery) do Shakespeare and Thomas use to support the impact of their stories? Use at least four direct quotations (two from each text) as supporting evidence in your essay.

Calibrated Reciprocity, Self-Disclosure, and Vulnerability in the Classroom

Sara Lawrence-Lightfoot, sociologist and professor at the Harvard Graduate School of Education, writes in her book *Respect* (1998) that her sister, "an educator, artist, and priest, also uses stories to nourish the I-thou connections" between students and teacher. She shares her sister's words:

> A child comes to school on Monday morning, comes to our circle of five-year-olds with the news that he has fallen off his two-wheeler. He shows us his Band-Aids of courage. Hands spring into the air. Everyone has a story to tell. Some are about

two-wheelers, others are about falls and scrapes, some are about car accidents, still others seem to be unrelated to the original story told, but I am sure by the child's urgency to tell it, now at this moment, that it is related in some way. It has touched my store of memories too, and I tell the children my story. (113)

This learning moment—in which teachers and students find common ground—is reminiscent of Hawkins' philosophy. High school English teacher Gregory Shafer similarly explores self-disclosure in an article for the National Council of Teachers of English:

It all began with an apology. I had missed a week of class after the death of my sister, and when I returned . . . I wanted to explain why I had been absent. It was an incredibly poignant moment, filled with pauses for tears. . . . A litany of questions were asked, followed by people adding their own stories. Deshauna had lost a brother to a drive-by shooting, and Langley had suffered the death of an uncle killed while in prison. Andy, a veteran of Iraq, had been traumatized by death as a vivid and ubiquitous part of his life. Suddenly, the plan for a cursory apology for being away had resulted in a classwide discussion about death and the ways it changes and even empowers those who experience it. . . . Many of the students who wrote about death, whether it involved a family member or friend, made similar allusions to the world beyond their personal loss. They discussed political injustice, racism, crime, and the failure of a system to protect the lives of those most vulnerable. (2017, 35–39)

Sharing elicits sharing. Authentic relationships require reciprocal vulnerability—not only an *I* and an *it* but a *thou*. If one person discloses their experiences to a listener who is repeatedly impersonal, and is never met with a give-and-take interaction, the sharer could experience a sense of shame and internalize the belief that their stories should become secrets. Why trust a listener with tender stories, or participate in a discussion or assignment, when it seems as though you are speaking into a vacuum? Genuine connection is a two-way transaction.

The instructional moments revealed in the excerpts shared here represent instances when instructors decided to share pieces of themselves as people, complexifying the I-Thou relationship.

This decision holds the potential to normalize loss experiences, exemplifying for students how to healthily cope with and talk about difficult emotions. It could stave off the potential that grieving students will feel othered when expressing their realities. But we should not take the decision lightly.

I shared earlier in this book that teachers should not compare their experiences to students' or make assumptions about students' thoughts and feelings. For example, it's problematic to say, "My dad died when I was ten, so I know how you're feeling about your sister," because loss is so contextual, and teachers do not have insight into the nuanced nature of a student's personal relationships. It is better to instead ask open-ended questions and bear witness to students' stories in a way that responds to the information they provide, rather than entangle assumptions born out of our own grief experiences. For example, one student shared with author and education thought leader Shawn Ginwright, "'When you are young like us, seeing someone shot and killed is a lot different than seeing someone die of cancer'" (2016, 50).

But when the story of one's loss serves the purpose of learning objectives, or is somehow related to a student's loss (e.g., Glenn's grief in a district impacted by suicide), there seems connective potential and poignant power in careful, intentional, controlled self-disclosures that humanize conversations about mortality. As Priscilla told me, teachers "have to be able to be a whole person" with a range of emotions, resisting the oft-internalized notion that they must, in the words of Ginwright, "be a role model to young people by showing them a 'trouble free' adult" (2016, 91).

In speaking with grief counselors throughout the writing of this book, I found that professionals unanimously advised teachers to check any impulse to share personal stories and consider whether the act of sharing would serve their own emotional needs or those of their students. Like all young people, bereaved students need boundaries in order to heal, and educators must keep those boundaries intact when navigating and negotiating self-disclosures in the classroom. Teachers' untended emotional work could further burden bereaved students. However, this does not mean that adults should not share stories of loss or vulnerability within appropriate bounds; the potentiality—

the energy quivering in those moments when we decide whether and what to share with others—remains in our toolbox for grief-responsive teaching. Following are some questions to consider when planning what stories you might share during class discussions.

Pause and Plan

When considering a moment of self-disclosure in the classroom, ask yourself:

1. What stories might I share in this moment?

2. Why do I feel compelled to share this anecdote? Would the disclosure make me feel better because of what I am going through, or is this solely for the sake of my student(s)?

3. What questions might arise from my sharing this story? Am I prepared to handle those questions? How does all of this connect back to our learning objectives or developmental goals?

4. If my supervisor were in the room, or a student's parent or guardian, would I still feel comfortable sharing this story and explaining its relevance?

Jeff Berman, college English professor and author of *Diaries to an English Professor: Pain and Growth in the Classroom* (1994), *Dying to Teach* (2007), and *Death in the Classroom* (2009), among many others, teaches postsecondary English courses on love and loss. I interviewed him to delve more deeply into the nuances of disclosure and the intersections between the personal and professional in classroom conversations about grief. He shared:

> Students do not ask me advice about how to live their lives, nor would I offer such advice beyond what is appropriate for a professor. They know that I cannot fix their problems. The best I can do is to create an empathic, nonjudgmental classroom in which they write about loves and losses and

reach their own conclusions. They teach and instruct each other, and they leave the classroom feeling a heightened connection to their classmates and teacher.

In my literature courses, I ask students to write reader-response diaries on how they feel about the stories we're reading. . . . The diaries, I state on the syllabus, should focus on students' personal responses to the novels.

Jeff regards himself as a "self-disclosing" teacher. "How can teachers encourage their students to write about love and loss without discussing their own experiences?" he wonders. But so, too, does he negotiate professional boundaries in his approach to students' personal writing. In response to a recently orphaned student's essay about saying goodbye to his mother, who battled addiction, Jeff shared:

How does one respond to this diary? The entry demonstrates Jacob's ability to connect Frederick's life [from *A Farewell to Arms*] with his own. Jacob helps us to understand why he did not wish to look at his mother's body, and we feel his anger and sorrow. . . . We also feel his grief over his father's death. Jacob did not need me to offer advice. . . . Nor did I tell him anything about his life that he did not already know. I would never presume to tell students how they should say goodbye to their parents or how they should feel about parents' deaths. Instead, I circled some of Jacob's grammatical errors (such as "made my brother and I") and apostrophe errors ("my parent's bodies"). I corrected a factual error: Frederick and Catherine never marry. Most important, I offered heartfelt praise of the diary's power and insights, remarking that Jacob ended with a signature Hemingway-esque line: "I try not to think about it"—a paradox in that the entire diary exemplifies Jacob's bold confrontation with a dark subject.

The three Rs of grief support are again relevant here, as we consider responding effectively to students' self-disclosures, negotiating our own, and supporting young people's intellectual growth in relation to curricular content. How we *recognize*, *respect*, and *respond* to students' expressions of grief—their social and emotional risk-taking in the safe spaces of our classrooms and caring relationships—has long-ranging implications for their self-esteem and processing of loss events, whether they feel a sense of ownership over their experiences or the need "to protect them," as Paterson writes in *Bridge to Terabithia* (1979, 75).

In his written feedback, Jeff strikes a balance between acknowledging content and technique in a way that rings true with a four-part framework I published on *Edutopia* (Collins 2019), partially reprinted here.

Responding to Students' Personal Narratives

Establish the Prompt

Consider the following writing prompt: *Tell me about a time when you demonstrated courage. Carry me into that moment: What did you hear, see, and feel? What did you say? What did you think? Was anyone present to observe your actions, or was your moment of courage more private, more internal?*

This prompt is one example of a way to spur personal narrative writing when working with middle or high schoolers. It is specific—inviting descriptive language, concrete nouns, dialogue, and so on—and it allows room for further constraints depending on learning goals, such as *Include in your piece two moments of dialogue* or *Re-create this moment in the form of a ten-line vignette.*

It is also vague enough to allow each writer the freedom to choose what area of their life most needs telling—that story on the tip of their tongue. As an added bonus, it is asset-based, encouraging writers to think metacognitively about a time when they rose to a challenge, cultivating positive meaning-making (Cain 2015) in students by inviting them to revisit memories that exemplify their resilience and fortitude.

Placing narrative emphasis on courage rather than on adversity provokes a story arc that frames the writer as rebounding—an important component of a growth mindset.

Acknowledge the Personal and the Academic

It's crucial to consider the ways in which students are opening their minds and hearts in personal narratives and to honor that vulnerability on the page. Because vulnerability can feel uncomfortable, and because writing assignments are most often rooted in curricular learning objectives, some teachers might feel inclined to respond only to the technical elements of a piece—correcting grammar, honing narrative flow, or tackling structural organization.

However, to catalyze the potential for social-emotional development inherent in personal writing, it is crucial to include in feedback an acknowledgment of students' stories—the content of their work—whether that content is funny, exciting, or heartbreaking.

Because self-disclosure can feel risky for students— even if their work does not seem explicitly or objectively vulnerable to teachers—acknowledging their sharing before delving into the realm of technical critique will empower their writing process.

In the first sentences of your response, thank the student for their story. Relate to their words by using statements like "This experience must have been very meaningful," or "I appreciate how honest your writing is about this topic." Restate the heart of their work in an original way.

Edit Through a Story-Driven Lens

Tending to the tactical elements of writing through a story-driven lens, in which student and teacher have the overarching purpose of the story in mind, catalyzes the natural attachment students have to their narratives.

In each of the following examples, the teacher's suggestions are tied to the student's larger message:

- Because this personal narrative is celebrating the life and legacy of your grandmother, it would be wonderful for readers to "hear" her voice on the page. Could you include two additional moments of dialogue in your narrative, so that readers can get an even deeper sense of her character?

- Your personal narrative about losing in this sports tournament highlights important themes: challenge, resilience, and resolve. Rather than address the lessons you learned from this loss in one body paragraph, try organizing your piece into three shorter supporting paragraphs, each dedicated to one of the three takeaway lessons that you learned. This will differentiate your ideas for readers and allow them to learn alongside you.

Teaching and editing with a story-driven lens taps into writers' intrinsic motivation.

Quote Student Work

At nearly every level, language arts teachers ask students to use direct quotations from texts to support their claims and arguments. The same strategy holds true for teachers' responses to personal writing.

Author Marc Jaffe says of his favorite teacher's class, "'You weren't just writing poetry. You were a poet'" (Daddona 2018). When teachers weave salient quotes from student work into feedback, writers see their words anew, through the lens of their teacher-reader.

Responding to personal narratives using analytical strategies that one might bring to a piece of great literature encourages writers to see themselves as personal essayists. Feeling their work is valued, students will then be more motivated to revise and refine their words. And teachers will learn more about their students' life experiences as they work with those students to make real the power of personal storytelling.

In Figures 5–1 through 5–3, you will find three pieces of writing composed by teen authors from around the world, originally published on the global writing education platform Write the World (https://www.writetheworld.com). Each piece engages the theme of loss in some way. Consider, as you read the voices of these young people, how you might apply the four-part framework to your own written feedback. What would you say to these students, using a grief-responsive approach? Importantly, some of these pieces are fictional, while others may not be. Often, when we receive students' work, we don't have the context needed to make that determination. Does that matter? How might—or might not—background info influence your feedback on pieces such as these? Practice in the spaces provided.

Title: **A Smile in the Stars**
Author: **Kaitlyn**   Age: **14**

Moss tickles my hands that play with a loose board that I try my best to fit my pudgy fingers through. My feet are cold as my toes dig themselves into the warm dirt that begins to coat my bare toenails. Every bone in my body seems to be holding its breath as a gust of wind pummels through my jacket that feels like nothing but a t-shirt. But still, I stay gripping onto my rickety post.

Everything is silent except for the hum of the crickets and the sonorous sound of trickling water. Tumbleweeds infest our countryside and it seems as though the snow queen had a visit as patches of ice are sparsely scattered throughout the fields. Our cows are inside as they can't stand the cold and so are our chickens, all who refuse to lay eggs as if they were plotting a revolt. Our farm is small. Maybe around half the size of a usual farm but granted, I hadn't seen many farms nor never traveled very far.

And as much as I thought it to be "dull" and "too old-fashioned," it was my mother's pride and is my family's remaining home. We all live in the big wooden home on the hill with a yard speckled with wild dandelions and littered with bugs and weeds that nobody bothers to pull. My father built the home out of wood from our trees just after my second birthday. Now I am fourteen and the building still stands radiantly in the sun. But now, it is nighttime and the home no longer shines in the spotlight. It is only an amorphous figure in the distance.

"Kai," I hear a faint call from behind me and the soft sound of footprints, "why are you up here so late?"

"Thalia, is that you?" I make sure not to fall off of my place on the fence as I turn around, facing my eight-year-old sister. "Does father know you're here?"

"I told him I needed apples," she says in almost a whisper, "but I knew you'd be up here too."

"Yea, yea," I call, though I crave seclusion for just one more second, "I'll be down in a bit so you can stay too. Come on, let's look at the stars."

I watch Thalia's tiny chin raise as she points her little face towards the sky. My eyes aren't fixed on the stars but on my little sister who's mouth begins to open in astonishment. I can feel a laugh brewing deep in my stomach. We had seen these stars a thousand times before and yet she looks as though this is her first time. Her hair caresses her shoulders and her navy blue jacket flutters behind her. Immediately, my overprotective side jumps at the opportunity as I throw my only sweater around her shoulders.

"Kai," she says my name and I barely recognize it, "*Is mum up there?*"

I almost cower away at the question and I look away. I don't want to tell her that she was buried in the graveside a year before she was born or that my father lost every single photo of her in the great wildfires that same year.

"Yes," I say, improvising, "see those stars."

A pattern of stars seem to emerge from nowhere in a crescent moon shape.

"That's her smile and those are her eyes. Her incandescent aqua blue eyes."

And I look back at my sister in whose eyes I see fragments of my mother.

(continues)

(continued)

Practice response: *If I were to respond to Kaitlyn's writing, I might say . . .*

Figure 5–1   Student Work: Sample 1

Title: **the beats i wish i could save**
Author: **Payton**   Age: **15**

i stare at her through the glass. in a daze, she tries to move her stiff blue nail, yet fails. a few coughs bring her face to her chest in pain. her strength is gone. it left a long time back. the bed she lies in will take her to a place far from here, she knows that. the white color she sees will be the last she knows. the tubes that try to save her will not be of use. the joy she once drank has left a dry lip on her face. the hope she once held will slip from her grasp soon.

  i yearn to break the glass in front of me and rush to her aid. the blue on her skin has reached her ears. i can see her brown curls and her jade green eyes. she wants me. she needs me. and yet they hold me back. i scream, i pound the glass in hope of its fall. i grab a chair and thrust it at the one wall that keeps me from her. i rush to her side and wrap her in a hug. she is cold. too cold.

i try to look at her jade eyes, but they close as i call her name. her limbs are stiff as i hold her. there is no way that this can be true. my mind is blank with hurt as i feel her chest. her heart has no beat. it's gone. she's gone. i do not know what they did to me next, all i know is that i still hear her name in my screams. i still feel her pain in my tears.

but most of all, i still feel her beat in my heart.

Practice response: *If I were to respond to Payton's writing, I might say . . .*

Figure 5–2   Student Work: Sample 2

Title: **the things we love**
Author: **Nimota**   Age: **16**

I held Rebecca's hand as she kicked and jumped and squealed with laughter whenever the waves touched her toes. It was her first time at the beach in months. It was rare for her to be strong enough to leave the hospital. I remember how pale and breathless she was just a few weeks ago and my heart breaks again. She didn't deserve this pain—no child did. But it would be over soon.

"Daddy look!"

I looked over to where she was pointing. A small orange starfish had washed onto the shore. I smiled and followed Rebecca as she ran to pick it up. Her face was stretched in an excited smile as she stared at her glistening new find. She looked up at me with big, pleading eyes.

"Can we keep it?", she asked.

I knelt in the sand and gently pushed her light hair away from her eyes.

"I don't think we can sweetie. It belongs in the sea."

"But I love it! And I'll take care of it, I promise."

I looked away and paused trying to control my voice.

"I know sweetheart . . . but sometimes we have to let go of the things we love."

Practice response: *If I were to respond to Nimota's writing, I might say . . .*

Figure 5–3   Student Work: Sample 3

Write and Reflect

When has the topic of loss or grief arisen previously in your curricula or classroom discourse, and how did you respond? What worked well, and what might you do differently next time?

As you consider your curricula for the forthcoming semester or year, do you foresee moments when discussions of grief may manifest? How can you prepare to structure those opportunities more mindfully? How might personal or analytical writing, mentor texts, and the I, Thou, and It and Text-to-Text, Text-to-Self, Text-to-World frameworks influence your pedagogies? How about personal-care permission slips or planned self-disclosures? What role does storytelling play in your curricula, and how do you feel about navigating this line?

What if I Mess Up?

Repair in Caring Relationships

Relational trust is built on movements of the human heart such as empathy, commitment, compassion, patience, and the capacity to forgive.

—PARKER J. PALMER, THE COURAGE TO TEACH

When we were children, we used to think that when we were grown-up we would no longer be vulnerable. But to grow up is to accept vulnerability. . . . To be alive is to be vulnerable.

—MADELEINE L'ENGLE, WALKING ON WATER

the takeaway from this chapter is both simple and challenging: Don't be afraid to revise.

Because grief work is inherently hard and makes us vulnerable, we often approach it feeling wobbly at best. Sometimes we say too much. Sometimes we say too little. Sometimes the fear of saying the wrong thing stymies our practice, and we slip into silence.

These are natural occurrences as we work to find—like Goldilocks—the balance that is just right.

In Chapter 4, we looked at miscommunications that well-intentioned teachers might make during grief work. As you read this book, you might feel a gnawing discomfort; moments may come to mind, from work or life, that nag at you—times when you felt you said or did the wrong thing while supporting (or not supporting) someone who was grieving.

I have these moments and memories, too.

But we must remember the redemptive potential for, and importance of, recalibration. We can resolve to make revisions when we feel that our first responses to grieving students were misaligned.

The first step, drawing from mindfulness practice, is to hold space for our own discomfort and accept our perceived mistakes without judgment. Perhaps you remember a silence that you wish you had filled, or a platitude you wish to retract, or a time when you could have shown up for someone but didn't or were overeager and could have backed off. Attunement in the face of grief is always subjective and evolving—shaped by the behaviors of students and teachers, each carrying their own contexts for approaching (or avoiding) the challenging entity of loss. Stigmatized or disenfranchised losses, meaning those silenced or not recognized in community—the death of a parent to suicide, a brother to addiction, a sense of future to an acquired disability, a vision of family to a miscarriage or infertility—enshroud grief support in further uncertainty because Western society conditions us not to confront these topics but rather to fear them and thereby perceive others actively grappling with them as "other." We do not often have the practice required to lend us agility in the face of grief support, so our shakiness is understandable.

That understanding can translate into action by way of apology.

Rather than lose ourselves in shame or discomfort, avoid the person we no longer know how to talk to, or repeat our initially problematic behaviors, we can be open and honest. We can have the direct and difficult conversation. We can expose and articulate our own learning and admit that we don't have the answers. And, through these actions, we can heal ourselves and others.

Why Apologies Are Hard

Our perceived errors in grief support often come from internalized insecurities around mortality and expressions of loss. How have our parents, teachers, friends, and partners responded to themes of mortality throughout our lives? How have we been met, heard, and supported (or not supported) during our own adversities? What losses, or fears of losses, or fears of our own mortality are we holding, and how do these harbored concerns drive our gut-centric responses to others' losses—before our prefrontal cortices kick in?

When we have a visceral response, a retractive reaction, to another person's expression of loss, what is the origin of our actions? Often, apologizing is challenging because it requires us to confront the uncomfortable truths that we hold within us—our own feelings of fear, regret, shame, and pain. Our own feelings of being let down. The transience of the lives around us, including our own.

In a landmark *60 Minutes* interview between Oprah and renowned trauma expert Dr. Bruce Perry, Oprah implores practitioners working with young people who are exposed to chronic stress, loss, and trauma to ask, not "What's wrong with you?" but "What happened to you?" (Winfrey 2018)—a shift in perspective that has become a refrain throughout much trauma literature. But if nobody has ever asked us what happened to *us*, we're not likely to ask another person. We may not even know our own answer. If this is the case, then when we respond to a grieving student in a way that we are not proud of, we risk sabotaging ourselves—asking, "What is wrong with me?"—and our hurtful actions might cause children to wonder what is wrong with them, too. In such a scenario, the root of our discomfort remains unresolved; we further silence ourselves and others because of a habituated impulse to retreat from pain, and we risk losing opportunities to learn. This is what happens when fear runs the show.

Taking Oprah's cue, then, growth begins by asking, "What happened to me?" Until we explore our inner terrain as it relates to themes of loss, we will not have full control over our actions and reactions with students. The writing prompts appended to each chapter of this book offer entry points into self-reflection, but there are many ways you might begin: freewriting or journaling, therapy, meditation, practicing iterations of the student-facing activities included throughout this book. Maybe you haven't experienced serious losses in your life and find it hard to empathize with the severity of a student's story. Maybe your life has been riddled with loss, and a student's grief response hits close to home. No matter where you fall on this spectrum, reflective activities remain relevant, laying the foundation for teaching from a space of self-awareness and intentionality.

Apology necessitates that we own our struggle, and owning struggle requires us to inquire about the root of that struggle. This is why saying, "I'm sorry," and meaning it, can feel so hard. But when we reframe our foibles in grief work as opportunities for learning about ourselves and others, we offer everyone grace. We make room for repair.

In Praise of Direct Communication

Oprah's interview with Dr. Perry affirms the potential for teachers—the safe place of school—to assuage the impacts of chronic stress, grief, and suffering. We know from this book that it takes only one person to offer the relational benefits that are the greatest antidote to, and preventative measure against, trauma. And we know that this power need not feel like pressure, but inspiration—that we do not have to be perfect or sacrifice our own well-being to help students, but we can offer attention and attunement, mindful boundaries, and authenticity in ways that align with our teaching philosophies and personas.

Direct communication is the hallmark of those things—the cog of reciprocity, symmetry, and wellness. "'When we've done something wrong, we tend to be self-focused,'" shared apology researcher Cynthia Frantz in *The Atlantic* (Urist 2016). "'You actually should be more focused on the other person, making sure they really believe that you get what you did wrong.'" What's more, apology gains heightened importance in the context of loss, as young people growing up in chaotic environments often don't receive the "interactive repair" necessary to maintain healthy attachments and "buffer" the impacts of trauma (Lunkenheimer et al. 2019, 353). By modeling repair as adults in an educational context, we lay a relational foundation and set an example that may not exist elsewhere in students' lives. Our decision to do so has direct implications on the internal working models with which students seek to understand themselves and others. Our example can challenge otherwise negative, internalized messages about whether and with whom it is OK to express "negative affect," or feelings of sadness, anger, and grief, and whether it is OK to have those experiences and needs met in a safe and supportive way (Pressley 2020).

The road to effective grief support is paradoxically me-centric. As discussed, we must do our own grief work in order to help others. That work allows us to shift from the "self-focused" lens Cynthia Frantz mentions to considerations of the "other person," acting in service of students without our own histories getting in the way.

To maintain appropriate boundaries when working with, or even broaching an apology with, teenagers, it's often most effective to focus not on disclosing the reason behind our actions but instead addressing the *what*. What we did the first time, what our actions made us think and feel, and what we wish we had said or done. Here are two examples and an invitation to write your own:

1. "Freddy, last time we spoke, you referenced your mom, but I neglected to check in with you about how you're doing since her diagnosis. I want you to know I am here to talk if that feels helpful to you."

2. "Zoe, I apologize if I seemed frustrated during our last conversation; I feel for all you're going through, and I want to be there for you. I'm frustrated that you have to deal with such hardship, not frustrated with you."

3. _____
   _____
   _____.

4. _____
   _____
   _____.

5. _____
   _____
   _____.

The Perils of Not Apologizing

Because grief work is often uncomfortable, and apologies are uncomfortable, it may feel easiest to allow our perceived mistakes to slide, telling ourselves we'll do better next time or that it's not our responsibility to handle a grieving student's situation.

However, there is risk in not revising our words and actions. As dance teacher Laurel Boyd shared, young people who are experiencing the heightened self-awareness of adolescence may have a "negativity bias" and internalize the cues that we project regarding their stories of loss. If we reacted in a way that we're not proud of, chances are the student felt uncomfortable, too, and may have anxiety about whether—and with whom—it is OK to speak honestly about grief. Students with histories of trauma may experience brain-based changes that can create devastatingly self-critical thought patterns and a hyperattunement to others' perceived opinions, meaning it is even more critical to prioritize direct communication and apology with students who you know to have a history of loss or trauma (Dillmann 2010; Souers and Hall 2016, 111).

Backtracking to share regrets and reemphasize intentions can stave off students' self-consciousness and patch what could be a powerful connection. Should you find yourself facing such a moment, return to the intentions for grief work you wrote at the start of this book. Consider your *why* and remember what happened to you.

Take a deep breath.

You are trying.

And by being explicit and clear, you will lead by example, showing young people that they, too, can take ownership of their actions and exhibit agency in the maintenance and restoration of relationships.

We are all vulnerable, L'Engle (2016) reminds us.

Apology pays homage to that fact.

Write and Reflect

Which apology are you most proud of making in your life, and why? Which apology was the hardest to make, and why? What is the most meaningful apology you've ever received, and what made it so effective? What was the least satisfying apology you've received, and what made it ineffective? Was there a time when you craved an apology but didn't receive it?

Look back at your responses and compile a list of ingredients for an effective apology. Encourage your students to do so, too.

Is It Possible to Teach Resilience?

Toward Hope: A Look at Grief and Growth

Imagining what might happen if one's circumstances were different was the only sure route to madness.

—AMOR TOWLES, A GENTLEMAN IN MOSCOW

But it is not bravery; I have no choice. I wake up and live my life. Don't you do the same?

—ANTHONY DOERR, ALL THE LIGHT WE CANNOT SEE

*G*rief is not an obstacle to overcome but a process to embrace, to endure, and with which to evolve. We know that it is not tightly contained by a five-step progression, nor is it a pathology from which to recover, but more fluid, cyclical, shape-shifting—a process that we can create space for and support one another through.

Many times, in my research for this book, I came across the word *grit*, made popular by Angela Duckworth's 2016 publication of the same name. It is one tenet of "character education" at KIPP charter schools, a focus of Paul Tough's 2012 text, *How Children Succeed: Grit, Curiosity, and the Hidden Power of Character*, and the subject of innumerable professional development offerings throughout the past decade. Most educators would agree: we want young people to persevere when encountering life challenges, and we would love to do anything in our power to support them in developing the skills needed to do so. But there is a problem with grit, at least as it has been interpreted and implemented in practice: it oversimplifies adversity, overlooks context, and places the onus of transcendence on students' shoulders in educational and societal systems founded on, and fueled by, inequity. Duckworth herself has acknowledged how her research has been oversimplified. And that oversimplification, when used to perpetuate marginalization, poses peril to students by masking the external elements that position some for overcoming challenges while others—students of color, those from low-income families, those who experience childhood maltreatment—face more hurdles no matter their gumption or resolve.

"How much grit actually makes a difference when nothing changes around you?" asks Ginwright in *Hope and Healing in Urban Education* (2016, 17). In the contexts of racism, poverty, or other inequality, implying or telling children to "toughen up," "power through," or "harness their grit" is a detriment. In the context of grief, "pull yourself up by your bootstraps" notions overlook the roots of contextually complex losses and place the responsibility of success on students' shoulders, perpetuating unhealthy messages about the compartmentalization and validity of hard feelings.

When faced with the aftermath of a drive-by shooting, Velada exhibited resilience, resourcefulness, and sorrow. No amount of grit education could have primed her for that event, nor for her responses to it, and neither would character development exercises assuage the PTSEs of Priscilla's students in foster care.

Promoting resilience does not mean praising students on the "flip side" of their loss, when they seem to outwardly achieve triumph over their trials. Instead, supporting the development of resilient learners in the face of loss means applying knowledge of development, well-being, and the tenets of trauma-informed care—safety, connection, and emotional regulation—to empower students to embrace both the challenging and heartening components of their lives; accept and express a range of emotions; and work to maintain or move toward a sense of future in the face of events that threaten to dampen one's dreams.

When we praise only stoicism or expressions of positivity, we subliminally signal that hard feelings are liabilities that should be suppressed. We risk complimenting an attitude that is largely performative—a guise put forward by a student who knows that being anything other than fine is frowned upon in our society.

Pema Chödrön wrote, "[Things] come together and they fall apart. Then they come together again and fall apart again. It's just like that. The healing comes from letting there be room for all of this to happen: room for grief, for relief, for misery, for joy" (1997, 9). To be resilient does not mean to be unfazed or unchanged. It means to embody grief and relief, misery and joy—what education scholar Parker Palmer refers to as the "opposite truths" (2010, 65) that we hold within us, that shape who we become. It means being honest with ourselves and with others.

But how do we reach this level of honesty and integration? How do we teach it in a safe, supportive, and scaffolded way?

We can start by creating a space in our classrooms, curricula, and caring relationships where we welcome and support opposite truths. By creating and earning a sense of safety and trust. Because, without trust, attempts at grief support feel like trespassing.

We can also do this through tangible techniques that seek to afford students relief from grief: mindfulness practice, memorialization, expressive writing, affinity communities, and flow-state activities (art, music, theatre, yoga, dance, athletics, academics, etc.) that seek to supplement students' challenges and infuse into their lives restorative, relational practices that counteract states of hyperarousal, dysregulation, violation, and pain by offering choice, creativity, and a sense of contribution.

Beyond "Om": Meditation Practice in Grief and Bereavement

Mindfulness—the act of paying attention, in the present moment, nonjudgmentally—originates from traditional Buddhist practices but gained secular attention through the work of Jon Kabat-Zinn, who launched the first Mindfulness-Based Stress Reduction (MBSR) program through the University of Massachusetts in 1979 (Greater Good Science Center 2021; University of Massachusetts Medical School 2014). Originally designed to aid terminally ill patients in hospitals by enhancing their ability to cope with physical and psychological pain, the success of MBSR spurred its adaptation and integration into the realm of business, where it was thought to enhance employee productivity (Congleton, Hölzel, and Lazar 2015). Soon after, the practice made its way into the field of education through such initiatives as Mindful Schools—a nonprofit organization that has trained over fifty thousand education professionals (Mindful Schools 2019)—and the scientific research backing its benefits supports wider integration.

Emotional regulation and impulse control, components of executive functioning, are attenuated in many students experiencing grief or working through trauma, because of the brain-based changes we explored in Chapter 1 (Ruedo and Paz-Alonso 2013). Students who struggle with executive functioning may be more prone to acting out in class, exhibiting anger, challenging authority, or acting on other disruptive impulses, which, in older students, could lead to self-destructive behaviors that pose greater and more perilous disruption to students' (and teachers', parents', and guardians') regulation.

Functional MRI (fMRI) brain scans suggest that consistent mindfulness practice has the potential to change brain structure. Researchers at Massachusetts General Hospital discovered in meditators increased gray matter in the hippocampus, the part of the brain responsible for memory and learning. They also found reduced gray matter in the amygdala, which is involved in the fight-or-flight response that is so central to chronic stress and trauma. A control group showed no alterations (Bhanoo 2011).

In 2016, researchers studied participants in an eight-week MBSR program and found strikingly similar results: "Demonstrable functional and structural changes in the prefrontal cortex, cingulate cortex, insula and hippocampus are similar to changes described in studies on traditional meditation practice," they reported. "In addition, MBSR led to changes in the amygdala consistent with improved emotional regulation. These findings indicate that MBSR-induced emotional and behavioral changes are related to functional and structural changes in the brain" (Gotink et al. 2016, 33). Consistent practice, even outside of a structured MBSR or other program, could catalyze similar behavioral and brain-based changes (Schulte 2015; Walton 2015).

There is anecdotal evidence that introducing mindfulness in the face of grief can be interpreted as an invalidation rather than an act of caring, in the way that grit and character education have clouded many education reform efforts. Megan Devine writes in *Huffington Post*: "In the mainstream language of mindfulness, if you would only change your thoughts, your grief would disappear. Any pain or trouble will be transformed if you think about it right. If you would only be here now, you would see that everything is okay, exactly as it is" (2014).

Additionally, there are students for whom mindfulness practice proves counterproductive: Sam Himelstein, a clinical psychologist and author who works with incarcerated youth, noted that the act of closing one's eyes could amplify a trauma response in some young people (Schwartz 2019).

Integrating mindfulness practice in a trauma-informed, grief-responsive manner therefore necessitates meeting students where they are, offering and encouraging modifications to practice, and scaffolding the integration of mindfulness in curricula with attention to language. Breathing exercises are not meant to erase justified grief, but to offer a coping strategy that students can use in moments of challenge. Ginwright notes that mindfulness, which he practices with youth in urban school districts, seemingly conflicts with a trauma context—accepting present conditions nonjudgmentally would mean accepting racism or other injustices nonjudgmentally—yet he believes in the physical benefits of the practice and is therefore thoughtful about the words with which he frames mindfulness in schools: "No amount of mindfulness will create access to quality housing and access to medical care in poor communities," he writes, but contemplative practices can help students "stay centered in turbulent times in order to make decisions, and lead from a place of compassion and love" (2016, 27). In other words, mindfulness invites students to access their upstairs brains.

Humans possess four kinds of brain waves—beta, alpha, theta, and delta (Herrmann 1997). We spend much of our days emitting beta waves, which help us stay alert and tuned in to the world around us. But we also emit beta waves in times of stress, anxiety, and hyperarousal, meaning that if we spend too much time submerged in their pool, we may begin to feel like we're drowning.

Alpha waves offer an antidote and are emitted when we are relaxed but aware—uninterrupted by outside stimuli (Miller 2019). Meditation promotes the production of alpha waves, which is why it induces a calming effect, even in small doses (Larson 2019). That calming effect, in turn, is associated with improved immunity, lowered blood pressure, and an increased ability to cope with pain. It dampens the inflammatory responses—in body and behavior—that we experience in response to grief or trauma.

In the classroom, making mindfulness a consistent component of students' routines introduces these alpha-wave states to support students' development of habits that promote effective coping. Dance teacher Laurel Boyd told me about mindfulness practices she uses:

> Breath work, meditation . . . even beginning class with a brief meditation, [a] collective breath . . . and ending class [that way]. We start together, we end together. Let's just find this moment of peace with each other. I think the earlier and more frequently we can make that a regular part of the school day, more students will become more apt to know what feeling

grounded looks like and feels like for themselves, and be able to ward off the more trauma-response activation that can sometimes take them out of class in a focused kind of way.

Educator and author bell hooks (2003) writes in a chapter titled, "This Is Our Life: Teaching Towards Death," about the ways in which education is perpetually focused on the future. By preparing students for someday—a future we can't possibly predict or envision—we necessarily forsake much of the now.

Breathing exercises are not meant to offer confrontation or escapism, but presence—focus. And their benefits are available to teachers, too. Consider practicing the following activities alongside your students. Use them as a starting point for integrating mindfulness into the daily rhythms and regulators of your classroom community.

Note: As you implement mindfulness activities in the classroom, keep in mind the following trauma-informed practices for yoga and meditation. To create an environment supportive of students who may be dealing with a variety of losses and traumas, try these approaches.

- *Narrate before you begin.* Tell students, in detail, what you will ask them to do during a certain activity as well as what you will be doing as the teacher. Eliminating uncertainty is important in a trauma-informed context, and giving students a sense of what to expect empowers them to sit out of any parts of an activity that might make them uncomfortable.

- *Maintain your space by staying in place.* Often, mindfulness activities give students the option to close their eyes. For students whose sympathetic nervous systems are activated in response to trauma, losing visual cues about their surrounding environment can activate or increase their trauma response. When students have their eyes closed, be sure that everyone (including you) stays where they are in the room. It's important that you

(continues)

don't move around and especially important that you
don't walk behind students or initiate physical contact
(by placing a hand on a student's shoulder to get their
attention, for example) while their eyes are closed.

- *Create inclusive classroom conditions.* Some students
  may be most relaxed when the lights are dimmed
  during a mindfulness activity, while other students
  could find this environmental change challenging.
  Unless you've checked in regarding students' individual preferences, refrain from altering the environment
  in ways that could activate students' trauma responses
  by changing or limiting the sensory information available to them; when the sympathetic nervous system is
  trained to scan an environment for potential threats,
  these sorts of changes can make what is supposed to be
  a calming environment stressful.

- *Offer adaptations.* It's good practice to offer multiple
  approaches to meditation and yoga exercises for
  students who may have a range of comfort levels,
  trauma histories, and abilities. For example, requiring
  students to partake in a yoga activity may exclude
  or "out" students who have invisible disabilities that
  preclude physical participation. In such an instance,
  meditation offers an alternative. At the same time,
  students who experience an increased trauma response
  during sitting meditation may find the physical engagement of yoga more helpful. Always ask students to
  listen to and honor their needs, and offer (and invite)
  adaptations to activities.

Bookend Breathing

As Laurel Boyd highlights, beginning and concluding class periods with collective breathing exercises is a simple but impactful way to introduce a component of mindfulness practice in the classroom. This activity offers a basic structure for doing so, which you can build out or expand on throughout the year.

Learning Objectives

This activity seeks to

- provide students with an awareness of breath and the calming power of paying attention to it,
- instill in them a mindfulness tool to use quickly, on the go, and
- establish a sense of continuity and routine.

PROCEDURE

1. Guide students through counts of four for the duration of five deep breaths (see following sample teacher narrative). If you choose to begin class in this way each day, students will become familiar enough with the process that you may choose to remain silent, encouraging them to count in their heads and breathing along with them.

2. At the conclusion of class, repeat this Bookend Breathing activity. You might ask each student to think of one word that represents their time in class that day and to repeat that word in their mind at each count.

Teacher Narrative

It's time to tuck away our phones, backpacks, and papers and rest our hands gently in our laps. We're going to start our class today practicing our bookend breathing. When I say, "Inhale," if it feels accessible to

(continues)

(continued)

> you, take a deep breath in while I count to four. Then,
> hold the breath for another count of four. Finally, exhale
> for a count of four. We will do this five times before we
> begin today's lesson. You are welcome to close your
> eyes if you'd like.

Mindful Reminders: A Treasure Hunt

OVERVIEW

This activity integrates into the daily routines of students and
teachers physical reminders that provoke mindfulness practice.
By selecting objects that represent mindful reminders, placing
them around the classroom, and establishing norms for the
mindfulness activities that students should practice when they
spot these objects, teachers can normalize and regularize present-
awareness focus and brain breaks in the classroom. Note that
students should not stop what they are doing (taking a math test,
for example) but rather use these objects as provocations for cen-
tering themselves in the moment when needed.

Materials Needed
- objects that will serve as mindful reminders, which could
  already exist within the room (the bookcase, the sink, a
  poster) or could be new objects, such as orange sticky notes
  hidden around the classroom

Learning Objectives
By practicing Mindful Reminders, students will
- establish regularity and familiarity in regard to basic mindfulness practices,
- be able to articulate and talk themselves through basic
  breathing exercises, and
- learn simple strategies for mindfulness practice to take with
  them outside of the classroom.

1. Assign three or more mindful reminder objects in your classroom and label them as a reminder for students (this label could be as simple as a sticky note, as mentioned earlier).

2. Determine with students what mindful actions these reminders will prompt—for example, deep breathing, or bringing awareness to the sensation of one's feet on the floor—and how frequently students should practice them (e.g., every time they spot the object versus seeking out the object when they feel dysregulated, etc.). Hint: With objects such as a clock or door, students can become silly and distract from class time given how frequently they encounter the object. Consider less visible reminders, or ask students to use more visible objects as cues for practicing mindfulness only when they need to, which is *not* every time they see the object in plain sight.

3. Check in with students throughout the week, semester, and year about their experience with mindful reminders. You may choose to switch up the objects or the actions that they prompt throughout the year, to keep the activity fresh.

4. Remember to participate in the actions that mindful reminders prompt, too!

Teacher Narrative

This year, we are going to practice a mindfulness activity called Mindful Reminders, which is similar to a combination of a treasure hunt and Simon Says. We're going to pick certain objects around the room that will serve as reminders for us to stop and practice our mindfulness skills. For example, every time you find an orange sticky note somewhere in the room, that's a sign that you should pause and practice five deep breaths. I will participate in this activity, too, and together we can remind one another not to ignore our mindfulness signs. We won't use these objects to stop what we're doing but instead to remind ourselves that we can access

(continues)

(continued)

> *mindfulness even while we are engaged in learning.*
> *For example, if you're taking a math test and spot one*
> *of our reminders, you can use it as a cue to relax your*
> *body and reorient yourself during your test.*
>
> *What objects do you think we should pick as*
> *our reminders and why? How should we label them?*
> *What should we do when we come across them? For*
> *example, we could practice a positive mantra, list three*
> *things we're grateful for, or practice our breathing.*

Body-Scan Bringdown

OVERVIEW

The body scan—a guided mindfulness activity that asks participants to tune into the sensations in their bodies from head to toe—is an integral part of mindfulness practice and a quick, adaptable way to de-escalate and center students in the classroom.

Mindfulness researchers have noted that mindfulness meditation body scans, which ask participants to notice and accept the sensations in each part of their body, activate different neural networks in the brain than relaxation-response body scans, which ask participants not only to notice and accept sensation but to *relax* the area of the body on which their attention is centered. For more information about these differences, please read "Mindfulness Meditation and Relaxation Response Affect Brain Differently," at the *Harvard Gazette* website (www.news.harvard.edu/gazette).

The following resources offer existing narratives for body scans in your classroom that you can use as is or adapt for your situation.

BODY SCANS FOR CHILDREN (APPROPRIATE FOR USE WITH FIFTH AND SIXTH GRADERS)

The following resources are available free of charge to stream through a computer or phone. Many also provide written transcripts you could print out and read aloud to students or distribute to students for whom auditory learning poses a challenge or who prefer to read the scripts themselves.

- "Body Scan for Kids" in *Mindful* (www.mindful.org/body -scan-kids/): This scan is available as an audio file to stream or a narrative script to read aloud.
- "Kids Meditation—Butterfly Body Scan," by MyLife (www .youtube.com/watch?v=56_8aK3cLEA): This video offers an audiovisual scan.
- "15/21 Days of Mindfulness Bootcamp—5 Minutes Bodyscan Meditation for Families and Classrooms," by Fablefy (www.youtube.com/watch?v=9A0S54yAgEg): An audiovisual body scan for classrooms and educators.
- "Body Scan Meditation by GoZen!" by GoZen! Online (www.youtube.com/watch?v=aIC-Io441v4): An audiovisual body scan meditation for kids.
- "Body Scan Meditation Techniques for Kids" (www .metroparent.com/daily/health-fitness/mental-health-self- care/body-scan-meditation-techniques-for-kids/): This *Metro Parent* article contains tips for introducing body scans to children.

BODY SCANS FOR TEENS (SIXTH GRADE AND UP) AND ADULTS

- The Calm app (www.calm.com): Though Calm is typically a paid app for use on computers or phones, at the time of my writing this, it also offers a number of free resources (audio files, printable downloads, etc.) specifically for teachers to use in schools, as well as free subscriptions for teachers, which you can access at the following link: https://www. calm.com/schools/resources.
- The Headspace app and website (www.headspace.com): Like Calm, Headspace is typically a paid subscription service; however, it offers free subscriptions to teachers for use in schools. At the following link, you can access free content available for streaming via a computer or phone: https://www.headspace.com/educators.

(continues)

(continued)

- The Mindfulness for Teens website (http://mindfulness forteens.com/guided-meditations/): This website offers a number of free audio files for streaming via a computer or phone, from meditations to body scans, targeted toward teens.
- "A Body Scan Script," *Whole Health for Pain and Suffering: An Integrative Approach*, on the University of Wisconsin's website (https://wholehealth.wiscweb.wisc.edu/wp-content /uploads/sites/414/2018/11/Script-Body-Scan.pdf): This is a free, printable narrative script that you could read aloud or distribute to students.
- The Mind Body Awareness Project: Mindfulness and Life Skills for At-Risk Youth (www.mbaproject.org/): The Mind Body Awareness Project site offers a number of free programs, resources, and trainings for educators interested in mindfulness, especially related to supporting youth in under-resourced communities.

BODY SCANS FOR TEACHERS AND STAFF

- Apps: As noted previously, Headspace and Calm offer free resources for educators, including materials focused on teacher self-care.
- Calm Classroom on Insight Timer: Calm Classroom programs offer body scans, breath work, and other audio tools for teachers. See "A Body Scan for Teachers" at https:// insighttimer.com/calmclassroom/guided-meditations /body-scan-for-teachers-2.

Memorialization

The class guinea pig died one morning before third graders entered their classroom, a teacher once told me at a professional development session one winter afternoon. Determined to dispose of the distressing evidence before the bell rang, she got rid of the guinea pig's body and welcomed her young learners into their space, sitting them down on the rug. "I have some very sad news," she told them.

Gasps were expected, even tears. But this teacher had not prepared for the overwhelming requests: "Where is he?" her students asked. "Can we bury him?"

There was consensus—amid their wiggling—that this was a brilliant idea.

So their teacher set to work: She arrived at school the following morning with a rock sealed inside a carefully closed shoebox and led her students single-file to the playground, where they buried what they thought was their beloved friend, sharing stories and memorabilia created for the occasion.

This story was met with uproarious laughter, mine included, when shared with a group of teachers over coffee one snowy Saturday. But I recall the tale, now, for the truth inherent within it: the truth that, no matter our age, there is unique power in recognizing loss in community.

I have heard stories from middle and high school teachers and students about schoolwide vigils and murals painted in honor of students lost to suicide; proceeds from school musicals donated in memory of a teacher; sports tournaments held in memory of a team member's parent; and assemblies, songs, apparel, and many other initiatives students and teachers have undertaken to celebrate the life and legacy of someone who touched their community.

My experience as a student was changed when my high school dance teacher offered to create a tribute performance in memory of my father. Every week throughout the fall semester of my sophomore year, we met to hone choreography with fifteen or so dancers, and at the end of the semester, we performed a commemorative piece against the backdrop of a slideshow featuring family photographs and quotes. Throughout the term, my fellow dancers and I met to debrief: Our teacher facilitated conversations about the emotional toll of the choreography, and we discovered that this was the first time many of us were not only dancing about something but *for* someone. Although the piece was framed as a tribute to my dad, other dancers shared their stories of loss and focused their energies on dancing for their close ones.

Together, we formed a mosaic of motion, exploring interiority and processing our thoughts and feelings individually and together. We were, in our own ways, third graders huddled around a swing set burying a rock in a box, finding solace in collective attunement, in the sense of purpose provided by contribution. We related with one another differently than before. And by the end of the term, we were bound by this experience of care.

Attachment is our first line of defense against loss and trauma (Di Ciacco 2008, 34; Bonanno 2009, 99). In fact, trauma often takes place when our efforts to reach out to others in the face of adversity are thwarted (van der Kolk 2014, 80). It makes sense, then, that the majority of memorialization practices across cultures involve nearness, communing, and storytelling. We make meaning by meeting loss together. We crave to know that we don't have to endure absence alone.

But then people disperse. A funeral ends, cards cease, and life returns to normal for all those beyond the immediate circle of the person who has passed. For young people returning to school, this can feel very lonely. There is a pressure to compartmentalize and assimilate while making some kind of internal sense of all that loss encompasses and of all that endures.

To bridge the divide, consider moments in your curricula or caring relationships when collective memorialization might allow students to meld the worlds of home and school. Always confer with the affected student first to gauge their level of interest; if they wish to keep their loss private, heed their wishes. Should they wish to pay tribute to their close one at school, however, ask them how. In the context of your relationship, what kind of effort might make sense? A bake sale for a favorite charity? Proceeds from a talent show donated to a local hospital? A tree planted for a former teacher? A moment of silence?

The act need not be large or even public to foster the benefits of recognizing loss in community, as long as the bereaved student is consenting, too.

Expressive Writing

Earlier in this book, we explored dialogue journals via Letters to a Listener, realizing that writing is a meaning-making activity. Humans are the only species to interpose a narrative arc on their lives in order to comprehend it (Gottschall 2012, xiv); stories are the medium through which we understand ourselves, synthesize our identities, perceive the world around us, and learn and relate to others. We learned that listening to or reading a story causes our brains to produce oxytocin, what Paul Zak termed the "moral molecule" (2012, 24)—a neurochemical that creates feelings of empathy and connection—and this is just one reason why the writing and sharing of stories holds the potential to counteract the isolation of trauma and loss: By writing our stories, we begin to extract significance, resonance, and lessons from our hardships, and by sharing those stories with others, and receiving others' stories in return, we braid together bonds of connection across difference. We understand what is uniquely ours and what experiences and emotions unite us. We gain confidence and even safety.

But the story must start with ourselves.

Expressive writing, akin to freewriting, is somewhat different from the reflective journaling encouraged in the activities listed previously, as it is intended not to have an audience. You ask students to write about their thoughts and feelings, using emotion words, without regard to spelling, punctuation, or other mechanics. The practice grew out of Pennebaker's late-twentieth-century research on expressive writing for the treatment of trauma, in which participants wrote about their traumatic memories, addressing the experiences and emotions that they often kept secret, not only from others but themselves. Pennebaker's study revealed that expressive writing led to improved social, psychological, and physical health, including improved lung, liver, and immune function (Pennebaker 2017; Baikie and Wilhelm 2005, 339).

Introduce students to the practice of expressive writing and its health benefits, but do not suggest they write about traumatic or loss-related memories; trust they will explore whatever topics feel most urgent in their inner terrain. Distribute personal journals alongside dialogue journals, and begin each class period with a five-minute private freewrite, encouraging students to track and record their trains of thought. Discuss the use of emotion words and "I am" statements. Normalize this practice by modeling it yourself, writing with students during designated times or discussing when and how you turn to expressive writing as a personal-care practice.

Grief Poems

Poetry is a powerful tool with which to combine memorialization and expressive writing. Because there are endless possibilities regarding topic, form, and approach, grieving students may find multiple entry points for exploring and communicating their feelings through poetry after a loss. Consider how you might offer mentor texts in your classroom, such as poems that entertain themes of loss or remembrance and that are appropriate for the grade level you teach (many poetry websites, such as www.poets.org and www .poetryfoundation.org, allow visitors to search by subject matter). Invite students to explore these poems and to write their own— whether for themselves, to share with family members and friends, or to use as an expression of memorialization. Here are some forms of poetry that may prove especially helpful:

1. **Definition poems** invite writers to complete open-ended sentences through poetry; for example, "Grief is . . . ," "Loss is . . . ," "Memory is . . . ," "Connection is . . . ," etc.

2. **Elegy poems** are written in remembrance, most often for a person, though some poets may adapt the form to remember a place, thing, or idea.

3. **List poems** might invite poets to share associations, memories, concrete physical details, or even dialogue, through poetic verse. A student might write an imitation poem in response to Wallace Stevens' "Thirteen Ways of Looking at a Blackbird," for example, such as "Thirteen Ways of Saying Goodbye," or "Thirteen Ways I Remember."

4. **Found poems** might allow students to take a piece of writing from a loved one who died and adapt the writing to create a poem using that person's words.

5. **Odes** are a form of writing that allow students to compose a poem directly in memory of a person, or to write about a broader topic that still incorporates resonant themes or experiences (e.g., "Ode to Nana," "Ode to Summers on Nana's Porch," "Ode to Family Traditions," etc.).

To learn more about poetic forms and devices, or to share your or your students' grief poems, check out The Grief Poem Project on www.GriefResponsiveTeaching.com.

The Power of Affinity

In his seminal text, *The Body Keeps the Score*, van der Kolk writes about Trauma Drama, a theatre group dedicated to engaging youth who are suffering from post-traumatic stress in psychodrama—theatre activities and productions that support social-emotional and psychological growth (2014, 336–48). He writes about the power of group synchrony—the attunement one feels with others when collaborating toward a common goal—and the importance of feeling needed, of being a necessary and cherished component of a larger whole.

His reflections resonate with Ginwright's facilitation of healing circles in urban school districts—groups of teens impacted by poverty, loss, and trauma that come together with Ginwright or another responsive educator to practice mindfulness and share stories about their experiences (2016, 12). Priscilla Kane Hellweg's work with foster youth at Enchanted Circle Theater, a nonprofit, multiservice arts organization in Holyoke, Massachusetts, similarly exemplifies the power of communing, practicing expressive arts, and working together for a larger purpose. Her programming also affords insight into the textured, multilayered network of connections that must come together in trauma-informed, grief-responsive care to create artistic and educational spaces within which youth can experiment, express, and grow. Priscilla shared:

> We do a lot of work with youth in foster care who deal with loss on multiple levels, in profound ways. We have a program called Youth Truth, which is a performance ensemble of youth whose lives have been impacted by foster care, and we are in our eighth year of doing this. . . . These young people are dealing with so much trauma and loss and grief, and have for so long, without the supports in place to be able to help them process it. Not that it's ever easy to live with grief and to process it, but it's harder sometimes than other times. And so, when we're working with the youth in Youth Truth, one of the

things we're trying so hard to do is really create a wraparound
system so that there's constantly somebody on overwatch
who can take that time to kind of read the room—in addition
to the people who are facilitating, in addition to the people
who are there on call at any time if somebody needs an intervention or some time to just chill in somebody else's room.

Anticipating that level of trauma, we build in ways of supporting them, and even still, sometimes something is triggered
and somebody lashes out and says something very hurtful to
somebody else, and then that affects something else.

With her staff, Priscilla actively considers the question "With grief
and trauma in education, what are the proactive things we can do to
support students?" She finds, most often, that learning how to "build
the wraparound systems" that cater to the whole of students' cognitive, emotional, and relational needs sets her and her students up for
meaningful and productive learning.

Courage Clubs

Priscilla's work with Youth Truth and van der Kolk's overview of
Trauma Drama reveal the intricacy and possibility of dedicated
programs for youth who are experiencing trauma. Similarly, bereavement support groups, summer camps for children who have
lost a parent, and many other affinity spaces across the country and
around the world offer young people the chance to meet other young
people who are experiencing grief.

Yet Ginwright's healing circles exemplify that the benefits of
affinity need not be limited to programs outside of school. You, or
your school counselor, psychologist, or other support professional,
can create these communities within your student body by forming a
courage club for anyone impacted by some iteration of loss.

Courage club curricula can include many of the pro-resiliency
practices highlighted in this book: meditation and mindfulness;
yoga, theatre, dance; expressive writing and craft projects; circles of
sharing; acts of memorialization; reading, writing, and book discussions; poetry and spoken word; fundraising for a loss-oriented cause.

While you can tailor the programming to your specific schooling
context, subject expertise, support staff, and student body, the power

of affinity and relational support by both peers (lateral) and mentors (linear) validates courage clubs as an extracurricular option for supporting grieving students at school. Activities need not relate to loss, and they should not put students on the spot to express their experiences, but rather they should foster group synchrony and community attunement that may, in time, allow for direct explorations of loss experiences by way of writing, sharing, creating, or other collaborative endeavors.

Professional Development Extension

In the next chapter, we will explore secondary traumatic stress (STS) and the need for teachers to feel similar support from a community of colleagues. You can modify the courage club model for a professional development context in which teachers participate in *Learning from Loss* groups dedicated to discussions of practice surrounding trauma-informed, grief-responsive pedagogies, the challenges they are facing in navigating loss in their classrooms or curricula, and so on. Using the reflection questions at the end of each chapter in this book offers a starting place for writing or talking about professional experiences in a community of colleagues.

Finding Flow

Self-determination theory, a framework created by Desi and Ryan for understanding intrinsic and extrinsic motivation, suggests that humans function best when we feel a sense of "autonomy, competence, and relatedness" (Niemiec and Ryan 2009). Loss and trauma threaten each of these tenets. Because trauma is often born out of experiences in which we feel immobilized (van der Kolk 2014, 99–100); lack the autonomy to change our circumstances; experience a perceived threat; or are isolated from others physically, socially, or emotionally, we lack a sense of control, efficacy, and worth. Loss can disempower and demotivate us.

Healing therefore takes place through actions, interactions, and activities that counteract disempowerment and reinforce attachment and agency (hence Bath's [2008] emphasis on safety, connection, and emotional regulation). Autonomy and competence connect especially to what Mihaly Csikszentmihalyi calls "flow state," a term from positive psychology used to describe those times when a person is so immersed in what they are doing—running, performing, painting—that the rest of the world seems not to matter; people will continue engaging in the activity simply for the joy that it provides (2014, 136).

Scientists posit that a sense of control is an important ingredient in creating this flow state which is especially poignant in a grief context. Control is at the root of our need for routine and consistency in the face of loss and at the heart of maintaining or regaining a sense of wellness during loss or trauma.

There are different flows for different folks. Whether practicing concertos or dribbling a basketball, trail running through snowy woods or poring over a chessboard, students will find flow in different places. They might gain from these activities both a temporary release from grief and the sense of competency and autonomy elicited by flow. Relatedness, too, may enter the picture if their flow-state activity takes place on a team or with a group, where students might find a sense of community and belonging as well as contribution. Supporting students' passions outside of the classroom, finding ways for them to share their expertise inside the classroom (by connecting passion projects to curricular content, inviting them to teach the class a favorite activity, etc.), and introducing them to new activities promote personal caretaking and bolster the likelihood that they will find and practice their flow state, transferring a positive experience to their sense of self in the face of loss.

A Note on Nature: Green Spaces, Blue Places

From the rush of a flowing river to the turf of a nearby soccer field, time spent in nature provides significant psychological and physiological benefits. Renowned neurologist and author Oliver

Sacks frequently took his patients to gardens, recognizing their miraculously calming effect on even his most challenging cases (2019). At the time when he wrote an essay titled "The Healing Power of Gardens," Sacks presented compelling anecdotes suggesting such an effect but did not have empirical evidence to back up his observations. Since then, however, numerous studies in psychology and education have revealed that nature proves especially helpful for people who have experienced trauma or who live in under-resourced communities. In 2020, researchers discovered that nature-based environmental education resulted in improved STEM skills and health-related quality of life (HRQoL) scores in students of color ages ten through fifteen who came from low-income backgrounds (Sprague, Berrigan, and Ekenga 2020, 198). One year prior, researchers revealed that nearness to water—"blue spaces"—resulted in increased happiness, higher levels of vitamin D, improved social relations, and psychological benefits for all people, including those who are grieving. In some cases, the benefits of being near water may even trump the benefits of spending time in other areas of nature (Hunt 2019). And in 2018, studies produced by the University of California, Berkeley, found that whitewater rafting trips significantly reduced symptoms of PTSD in both veterans and children from under-resourced communities. This impact, researchers revealed, is attributable to the feeling of *awe*: "Their findings, reported in two articles published in the journal *Emotion*, suggest that awe—as opposed to joy, pride, amusement, contentment and other positive emotions— is the singular sensation that goes the furthest in boosting one's overall sense of well-being," wrote Yasmin Anwar (2018).

But one does not need to attend a forest kindergarten or vacation in the Grand Canyon to reap these psychological benefits. Finding one corner of the schoolground or neighborhood in which to attune to nature can begin to foster this sense of connection, attention, and calm. Use the following sensory immersion exercise to enhance students' connections with nature.

Nature Noticings

Overview

Nature Noticings is an immersion activity that facilitates awe *and* academic engagement. The following instructions invite you to create experiences for students to connect with the natural world, reap the benefits of that connection—as explored in this chapter—and channel their noticings into classroom curricula across subjects.

Materials Needed

- Notebooks or paper
- Pens or pencils
- Access to the outdoors or ways of connecting alternatively with nature (Youtube videos, images, etc.)

Learning Objectives

By participating in this activity, students will…

- learn to attune to nature in new ways,
- practice mindful awareness through the senses,
- create conditions for experiencing awe, which we know to be important in well-being,
- document their observations,
- connect and extend observations through curricular content, and
- practice a potential coping mechanism.

PROCEDURE

1. Invite students to take out a piece of notebook paper and create five columns, one for each of the five senses: "See," "Hear," "Feel (Touch)," "Taste," "Smell."

2. Ask students to find a spot to observe nature. Ideally, this will happen outdoors; however, if students do not have direct access to the natural world, they may find alternatives such as listening through or looking out of an open window, or looking at Google Earth or a nature-based YouTube video.

3. Request that students spend five (or more) quiet minutes observing the natural world through each of the five senses, recording what they notice in the appropriate columns on their paper.

4. Invite students to use the back of their paper to reflect upon their nature immersion by recording what their observations made them think, feel, or wonder.

Assign this activity periodically throughout the semester to create a sense of routine or to connect the practice to classroom assignments. If you teach poetry, for example, ask students to pick five bullet points from their sensory lists to incorporate into a nature poem. If you teach science, ask students to pick three bullet points that they would like to explore further or learn more about, as a jumping-off point for student-driven inquiry. Connecting curricula with experiences that promote social-emotional wellbeing threads together grief-responsive teaching and students' academic engagement.

Contributory Activities and the Power of Choice

Throughout this book, I mention empowering students' agency through choice activities. Choice affords a sense of control that is especially helpful in a grief context. Whether allowing students to pick which book they would most like to study during a literature unit, or building into class periods blocks of time for students to choose from a selection of academic or regulatory activities, giving students a say in how, where, or when they learn compensates for what may prove to be chaotic home environments in which such choice and control do not exist. Similarly, contributory activities—such as the memorialization efforts mentioned earlier; a group community service project; or a team sport or collaborative theatre, dance, music, or art production—foster a sense of competence, attunement, and synchronicity with others that is restorative in a grief and trauma context (van der Kolk 2014, 335–48). Many school activities inherently cater to choice, agency, and contribution, but taking a look at curricula through this lens and finding ways, however small, to structure such activities more formally, enforces their impact on the lives of students who are grieving.

Resilience in Perspective

When problematizing grit and considering the possibility of promoting resilience in youth, it is important to note that many people experiencing bereavement exhibit healthy adjustment and do not require psychological intervention. George A. Bonanno, a grief researcher, professor of clinical psychology, and chair of the Department of Counseling and Clinical Psychology at Columbia University's Teachers College, explains in *The Other Side of Sadness: What the New Science of Bereavement Tells Us About Life After Loss*:

> Bereavement experts have long doubted the resilience of people who endure the death of a loved one. . . . However, research has continually shown that many children cope extremely well with adversity. Even if we narrow our definition of resilience so that it includes only those at-risk children who turned out healthy in all the important areas of adjustment, on balance we still find unexpectedly high numbers (2009, 51).

While some individuals experience complicated grief—a term used to describe a more pervasive, chronic response that often requires psychological intervention—this research should reassure educators that many students hold the potential for emotional adjustment and psychological integration of loss experiences. That said, we cannot overlook the structural inequities—poverty, racism—that threaten this adjustment. We cannot rely on students' inherent resiliency to ensure their ability to triumph over trials, nor can we affix this process to some kind of fixed character trait.

Instead, we can work to instill or restore students' internal locus of control—their sense of competency in, and agency over, their lives, and in turn, their sense of future and intrinsic motivation.

We can offer them safety and support, community and synchrony, and opportunities to fuel their thoughts, feelings, and experiences into healthy outlets that promote well-being. We can bring into conversation the inequities that bind our society—for although death is sometimes regarded as "the great equalizer" (Albom 2007, 51), even in loss we are not equal. We can work to fight those systems of oppression that perpetuate inequity.

And we can decentralize grit, focusing instead on emotional regulation and resiliency, listening to and learning from our students most of all.

Write and Reflect

When you think about the composition of your current classroom, what do you consider the most significant challenges facing your students? What are the biggest barriers to resilience in their personal lives or in the context of your school district? When you think of your students, what keeps you up at night and why?

Next, make a plan. Think about your classroom routine, and consider when you could feasibly integrate mindfulness practices, expressive writing, or the other strategies addressed in this chapter. Sketch out a calendar and insert designated times to discuss and practice these strategies with your students.

CHAPTER

8

What if I Can't Do This?

Compassion Fatigue and Secondary Trauma: Protecting the Teacher's Heart

Caring for myself is not self-indulgence, it is self-preservation, and that is an act of political warfare.

—AUDRE LORDE, A BURST OF LIGHT: AND OTHER ESSAYS

Our deepest calling is to grow into our own authentic self-hood, whether or not it conforms to some image of who we ought to be. As we do so, we will not only find the joy that every human being seeks—we will also find our path of authentic service in the world.

—PARKER J. PALMER, LET YOUR LIFE SPEAK: LISTENING FOR THE VOICE OF VOCATION

"I have taught here more than thirty years—the very best job in the world," writes Penny Gill, a European politics and political philosophy professor at Mount Holyoke College, in Sam Intrator and Megan Scribner's anthology, *Teaching with Fire: Poetry That Sustains the Courage to Teach*:

> It is a profound privilege to spend my days with the gifted young women I teach. Coming from many continents, they bring the world into my office. I am moved by their intense desire to learn, their willingness to explore the world and discover their proper place in it. . . . But it is perhaps the students who are stuck or in deep pain who draw me in most deeply—my work with them is hidden behind my office door, where we sit in two big blue wing chairs and try to find the 'next step' in a difficult life (2003, 136).

Gill's words are a beautiful testament to the rewards of working with students in times of struggle. Teachers have the immense privilege of receiving students' "opposite truths"—their sorrow and sustained investment, their dreams and doubts, their hopes and fears (Palmer 2010, 65). Young people look to educators as guides in moments that feel tenuous or trepidatious, when their dreams are at stake. Yet they do not always realize that adults, too, hold opposite truths within them.

Secondary Traumatic Stress

One such opposite truth may be that teaching the whole of our students—receiving, respecting, and responding to all that they bring our way—is *both* a privilege *and* a potentially exhausting endeavor. Teachers are helping professionals, and it is critical to recognize the ways in which students' adversity can affect our minds and hearts in times of hardship. When we as practitioners are routinely exposed to others' traumas, we are at risk for secondary traumatic stress (STS), or compassion fatigue—a "natural but disruptive" reaction that parallels PTSD (Administration for Children and Families n.d.).

Secondary traumatic stress, like grief and trauma, occurs on a spectrum. Its symptoms may include (but are not limited to) feelings of saturation, isolation, and anxiety; depression, dissociation, and nightmares; and insomnia, physical ailments, and feelings of help-lessness or powerlessness (Administration for Children and Families n.d.). When students' losses and traumas poke at or reignite our own, we may experience "arousal and avoidance" (NCTSN Secondary Traumatic Stress Committee 2011, 2) and respond with a number of understandable but misaligned mechanisms: retreating rather than reaching out, or reacting with frustration, deflection, or denial (Haley 2015). Though paradoxical, these reactions often come from a place of caring, and they are grounded in biological responses as valid as those that our students experience after a loss. We care about young people's well-being, and we often feel powerless—a sense of learned helplessness—because we cannot change the circumstances that are causing young people pain.

Even if we know that listening, talking, and bearing witness hold the power to heal, that we have the agency to make a difference, "the essential act of listening to trauma stories may take an emotional toll that compromises professional functioning and diminishes quality of life" (NCTSN Secondary Traumatic Stress Committee 2011, 2). The students whom we care about can consume our consciousness and cause us pain. The profession that infuses our life with purpose may also leave us feeling powerless. We may burn out of once-meaningful relationships and perhaps our job as a whole.

But this does not have to be the cost of our caring.

Radical Reckoning

The first step in preventing and addressing STS is to tune in, non-judgmentally, to our own internal realities—the opposite, and at times uncomfortable, truths that we carry into the classroom. We can acknowledge the judgments we make and the irritations we hold when students' losses and traumas result in behaviors that challenge us. We can honor the impulse to avoid or shut down dif-ficult conversations about loss and grief. We can feel the unease in our stomachs when we wonder whether our words were effective, when we wonder whether to say any words at all.

We know that young people deserve not only our consideration but also our reconsideration. We teach because we believe in students' growth and change; their ability to evolve and adapt is central to the experiences of teaching and learning.

We also know that students' home lives and the contexts in which they learn impact their behaviors in the classroom. We are infuriated by the inequities that cause students' suffering, that stymie the dreams of some students more than others. We worry about young people's futures.

We know and do all of this because we want the best for young people. We want to do what we can to help them become their best selves, to head out into a world we will not necessarily witness, a world we can't predict, with the intellectual and personal skills required to excel, adapt, connect, and innovate, in whatever shapes or shades success looks like for them. We want them to live a life of happiness and meaning. This is not ideal.

It is challenging, though, with these as our intentions, to acknowledge within ourselves the symptoms of secondary traumatic stress— the desire to avoid a specific student or story; the frustration or feeling that grief work is not our job; the tug and tension that surrounds our attempts to balance content-based knowledge and state standards with social-emotional development; the desire, even, to hit snooze and skip work. "Who are we?" we wonder, once wide-eyed educators committed to making a difference through learning. Surely, we think, our younger selves would be ashamed of the thoughts and feelings that sometimes arise in us when we are learning from loss.

But these thoughts and feelings are signs of strength—symptoms of our investment and intentions. This I know.

They may feel, at first, like shame, which Brené Brown defines as "an intensely painful feeling or experience of believing that we are flawed and therefore unworthy of love and belonging" (Suttie 2016). Admitting our feelings of compassion fatigue as professionals takes a level of vulnerability that may lead to self-judgment, shame, or embarrassment. Because avoidance is a natural response to trauma and grief, and a symptom of STS, we may feel an impulse to avoid our feelings of STS as well as the students whose stories cause those feelings to arise in us. In speaking with teachers while writing this book, I heard stories of individuals so preoccupied—so invested—in a given student's loss that their all-consuming concern prevented them from getting through the school day. I spoke with teachers who left the profession after particularly painful tragedies left them reeling. I met teachers who left urban districts to teach in areas where privilege assuages susceptibility to STS.

Hearing these tales, the words of Velada Chaires rang, once again, in my mind: "You can't take them home," she told me. "You have to remember that you can't take them home."

There is ample literature investigating the unpaid emotional labor imparted upon teachers. For example, there is a gendered assumption that female-identifying teachers will be more sensitive, nurturing listeners, and students may turn to them more frequently than male colleagues to work through life challenges. Male administrators may similarly expect female-identifying teachers to embrace this unpaid social-emotional work (Flaherty 2018).

Educators with marginalized identities may find themselves mentoring students with marginalized identities; because affinity is so powerful, students with disabilities may seek the mentoring of teachers with disabilities; students identifying as LGBTQIA, the mentoring of openly LGBTQIA teachers; students of color, the mentoring of educators of color; and so on (Flaherty 2018; Shafer 2018). These connections are not bad—they can hold reciprocal meaning for teachers and students alike—but when the weight of this work shifts from privilege to burden; is not recognized in educators' compensations; creates inequitable demands between colleagues; consumes inordinate amounts of time (physical or mental); or is imposed upon an educator without explicit consent, teachers will be at a much higher risk for STS and burnout and will not have the capacity to help their students or contribute to their school communities in substantive ways.

When teachers are overburdened and emotionally unavailable, the schooling environment may compound trauma for all: teachers experiencing STS may react to a student with frustration, which then may exacerbate the students' trauma and result in behaviors that reinforce a teacher's STS. Just as the Connection Constellation activity in Chapter 4 highlights how interconnected and interdependent we are in our environments, including at school, so does the cycle of retraumatization reveal how students and teachers collectively and cooperatively influence the climate of the learning environment (see Figure 8–1).

Teachers who have histories of loss and trauma are at an increased risk for STS when the professional reflects the personal (Baicker 2020), which is why it is critical, amid the push and pull of grief work, to maintain balance and boundaries—buoys that stave off burnout and prevent this cycle of pain.

In the pages that follow, we will consider both preventional and interventional strategies for those times when students' losses consume us, realizing that, while we "can't take them home," there is much we can do—within appropriate educational and interpersonal parameters—to support students' well-being in times of grief while honoring our own needs, too.

The Cycle of Retraumatization at School

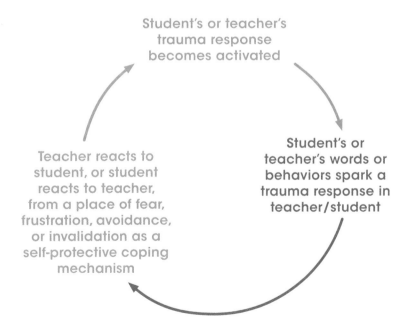

Student's or teacher's trauma response becomes activated

Student's or teacher's words or behaviors spark a trauma response in teacher/student

Teacher reacts to student, or student reacts to teacher, from a place of fear, frustration, avoidance, or invalidation as a self-protective coping mechanism

Figure 8–1   The Cycle of Retraumatization at School

A Growth Mindset for Grief Work

Neurologist Lisa M. Shulman writes in her book *Before and After Loss: A Neurologist's Perspective on Loss, Grief, and Our Brain* about a study conducted by researchers Jack Bauer and George Bonanno, who explored "how people talk during bereavement, differentiating between statements like *I can do things well* (which speaks to self-efficacy), *I do things well* (which speaks to self-management), and *I'm a good person* (which speaks to self-esteem)" (2018, 112).

People who made statements of self-efficacy "had fewer grief symptoms and better adaptation" (112). "Ironically," Shulman writes, "the best predictor of psychological health is the belief *I'm mostly good, some bad.* In other words, some negative self-evaluation is adaptive, while too little (*I'm not bad*) or too much (*I'm very bad*) is maladaptive" (112).

These findings speak to a familiar idea in education: Carol Dweck's conception of fixed and growth mindsets (2008). As a refresher, let's review their definitions.

Fixed Mindset

A fixed mindset leads us to believe that our capabilities and capacities are limited and unchanging. In such a mindset, we believe absolute statements such as "I'm horrible at math" or "I shouldn't even try to apply for a promotion, because I can't present in front of large crowds." With these beliefs, we become averse to risk and opportunity and can limit our own potential. We view constructive criticism as confirmation of our unworthiness. And we might spiral into jealousy, comparison, or self-criticism.

Growth Mindset

A growth mindset, on the other hand, allows us to believe that our skills are fluid and ever-changing and that we always have the capacity to iterate and improve. Through this lens, we view setbacks as temporary stumbles rather than permanent roadblocks. We might say, "I struggle with math, but I will get better with practice," or "Even though I don't like presenting in front of large crowds, I'm really excited for this potential promotion, so

I'm going to sign up for a public speaking class and apply for the opportunity anyway." With a growth mindset, the world is full of opportunities for lifelong learning.

If believing in our abilities to overcome loss helps us when we are grieving, how, then, might a similar growth mindset guide us in grief work at school, especially when we are feeling STS or disenfranchised grief?

The Three "Selves" of Social-Emotional Support

We must nurture three "selves" to stave off STS: self-efficacy, self-management, and self-esteem.

Self-Efficacy

Self-efficacy is the belief in our ability to act with competence. One could have situationally high self-efficacy ("I can absolutely recite Shakespeare's plays by heart") but low self-esteem ("Despite my impressive knowledge of plays, I am not smart or worthy of love"). A statement of high self-efficacy in the context of grief work might be "I can make time and space for my grieving students without sacrificing my own well-being."

Self-Management

Self-management is one's ability to take ownership of their actions, reactions, well-being, and executive functioning. In the context of grief work, self-care strategies are examples of self-management.

Self-Esteem

Self-esteem is one's belief in their inherent value as a person. In a grief context, a person with low self-esteem may feel inadequate, unworthy, and incompetent, which would impede their ability to connect with students who are struggling. Counteracting such tendencies with positive self-talk and healthy relationships can help restore a sense of esteem.

All of these "selves" influence not only the efficacy of our grief work but also the extent to which we are susceptible to the challenges of that work. It is critical to note that STS is natural, not necessarily within our control, and a serious experience that may require professional intervention and should not be reduced to a set of tips and tricks. However, creating within ourselves an awareness of self-efficacy, self-management, and self-esteem—tracking our own status in relation to each of these entities—offers a foundation for taking care of ourselves as we grapple with loss and as we cultivate our grief-work growth mindsets.

Write and Read Aloud

Make a list of five to ten self-efficacy statements, beginning each sentence with "I can." Hone in on those elements of grief work that most intimidate you or cause you pain, and practice reframing those entities through the lens of a grief-work growth mindset. Then, read your statements aloud (yes, really). Giving them voice allows them to grow.

I'll go first:

1. I can speak directly and compassionately about loss experiences—mine as well as others'.

2. I can avoid platitudes while speaking with those who are grieving, listening to (and asking about) their experiences instead.

3. I can approach grief work with calibrated vulnerability and purposeful self-disclosure.

4. I can be honest when a conversation or situation raises challenging feelings for me.

5. I can open conversations with other practitioners about their experiences with learning from loss.

6. I can recalibrate by reframing others' challenging behaviors as responses to the neurobiological and emotional experiences of grief. Context matters.

7. I can acknowledge the ways in which my first considerations of grieving students may be inaccurate and reconsider grieving students as they grow and change.

8. I can learn from my students' loss experiences and help them learn from them, too.

9. I can set boundaries and limits with grieving students to support my own wellness.

10. I can remember that I am not here to fix students' grief but instead to support their individual processes in my own ways.

When we practice cultivating self-efficacy—even, and especially, when we struggle to believe our own "I can" statements—we enforce our ability to learn from loss, and help others learn from loss, while keeping our own self-management in mind.

When in Doubt, Write It Out

Another strategy for self-management in the prevention and intervention of STS is freewriting. In the way that dialogue journals and Letters to a Listener, discussed in Chapter 3, promote storytelling and meaning making in students—integral processes in any loss experience—so does journaling help educators cope in times of challenge.

Ultimately, if we ignore symptoms of STS, and the acts of dissociation and avoidance so central to many individuals' trauma and grief responses, we risk worsening and prolonging pain and stunting learning and growth. It is not enough, then, to translate knowledge of health benefits into storytelling activities for grieving students. Because we know that receiving students' stories can increase teachers' likelihood for STS, we must simultaneously enact our own professional development practice, processing our grief—and grief work—through writing or other forms of reflection, communication, or storytelling to counterbalance and assuage the impacts of students' difficulties on ourselves.

You'll remember that freewriting is the practice by which we silence our internal critics, our innate editors, and place upon the page every word that comes to mind regarding a given topic (or no topic at all). Following our train of thought, even ending midsentence as our mind jumps to its next revelation, combines the kind of self-awareness that mindfulness practice promotes while indulging our thought process in a way that stands opposite to meditation but holds the healing power revealed by Pennebaker (2017) and others. When you recognize red flags within yourself—frustration, avoidance, sadness, a sense of being overwhelmed—take five to ten minutes, set a timer, and put pen to paper. Allow yourself to acknowledge, experience, and document the thoughts and feelings that arise for you in these moments, without judgment. Use emotion words (e.g., *angry, upset, confused, inadequate; inspired, encouraged, motivated, calm*). Only when we are honest with ourselves about grief work—and acknowledge our own loss experiences as they intersect with those of our students—can we enter the classroom with a more grounded, centered, and integrated approach to understanding, coping, and learning in community. So, too, can we simultaneously reap the physiological and psychological benefits of expressive writing as we process our own losses.

I Can't Just Breathe . . . Can I?

While writing is powerful and catalyzes well-being, it may not be enough to fuel you in times of trauma, grief, or stress. Bessel van der Kolk writes in *The Body Keeps the Score*:

> The act of telling the story doesn't necessarily alter the automatic physical and hormonal responses of bodies that remain hypervigilant. . . . For real change to take place, the body needs to learn that the danger has passed and to live in the reality of the present. Our search to understand trauma has led us to think differently not only about the structure of the mind but also about the processes by which it heals (2014, 21).

In Chapter 7, we explored the science of mindfulness and its role in supporting health and wellness in a grief context. Glenn Manning told me that, after his school district experienced a series of student deaths to suicide, he turned to a number of self-management mechanisms that offered him salve, mindfulness among them:

First and foremost, [it was critical to have] caring relationships of my own that enabled me to process the difficulty and the pain of what we were experiencing at work and to talk it through and problem solve. Outside of that, it was really important that I was attending to what is now called self-care. . . . Meditation practice was extraordinarily helpful in that time period, and exercise . . . really taking care of the mind and the body so that I could then go ahead and support others [and] have the bandwidth to do that. Preparing the ground emotionally . . . is critical.

Setting aside time each day to engage in the practices I addressed through a student-facing lens in Chapter 7—guided meditations and visualization, body scans, yoga practice—offers our nervous systems opportunities to engage in present moment awareness, or what van der Kolk has described as experiences that "terminate [our] continued stress mobilization and restore the entire organism to safety" (2014, 53).

When I am grieving or experiencing adversity, the last thing I want is for someone to tell me to meditate. I balk at what feels like an oversimplified, dismissive reaction to my problem. But when I am my best self, I sit down and close my eyes and center my attention. It feels like nothing, at first, yet when my session draws to a close, I feel invariably better. Not devoid of stress or pain, as that is not the point of meditation, but nourished from a brief reprieve, reaping the benefits of a calmer nervous system—benefits that, science has proven, linger long after the time of my practice.

So, in this instance, I will become *that* person and say, even if you roll your eyes: It is enough to breathe. Carve out time to slow down and center your focus to ground yourself in the face of grief work, whether in life or in school.

Professional Affinity: A Whole-School Approach

In addition to his many insights on the healing of trauma, van der Kolk notes that "trauma almost invariably involves not being seen, not being mirrored, and not being taken into account" (2014, 59). His explanation is eerily similar to the definition of disenfranchised grief, or grief that is complexified because it is not socially acknowledged (Thelen 2007).

Secondary traumatic stress, and the many forms of grief that educators may feel for and with their students, often fall into such spaces of silence—such disenfranchised grief. Jessica Lander writes in "Helping Teachers Manage the Weight of Trauma" that "building a culture of awareness" (2018) in which trauma and STS are openly discussed and normalized, among not only teacher colleagues but also school and district leaders, is a highly effective interventional strategy for schools.

Before we can tackle a problem, we have to acknowledge its existence. Before we can grieve, we must name our losses.

To truly revolutionize the school community in a way that supports grief work and trauma-informed instruction, improves teacher well-being, and staves off practitioner burnout, we must take a whole-school approach to learning from loss together. If a teacher's support of grieving students were neither siloed nor silenced but instead welcomed into conversations with colleagues and considered by school and district leaders, and if STS and self-care strategies were articulated among teams of professionals, how much healthier would our schools be for students and teachers alike?

A whole-school approach might include the following:

- professional affinity groups in which teachers discuss the challenges and successes of working with students who are experiencing grief or trauma

- a space and time each week when teachers meet to practice mindfulness together, with or without students

- open discussions, initiated by school leaders, about STS and the unpaid emotional labor teachers find themselves invested in

- advice from support professionals for school communities on the topics of grief and trauma, especially in the wake of a whole-school tragedy

- schoolwide conversations about personal-care strategies, balance, boundaries, and mental health

- regular conversations about—and initiatives to improve—safety, connection, and emotional regulation for teachers and students alike.

When a community is riddled with grief, it takes a team to support impacted students and a team to maintain teachers' well-being. This is especially true in vulnerable populations, as this story of Priscilla's practice illustrates:

Self-care for those in the teaching or facilitating role [is critical]. In the arts, it's not unusual to hear somebody say, "The arts saved my life." A lot of teaching artists come from having their own experiences [of loss and trauma]....The arts gave them their voice, the arts gave them their sense of future, the arts gave them a sense of understanding what their potential was. And it's not easy work being a teacher. This is a hard time in education, so teachers have to take care of themselves.

As a nonprofit organization, we are providing professional development for our staff in trauma-informed practice. We just took a two-day training. One day was on psychological first aid. . . . The people doing the training [were] people who work with first responders, helping them deal with the trauma that they're working with and also [going] into traumatic events after the first responders leave and [helping] the people [impacted]. The particular [professional facilitators] we were working with were there [at] the Boston Marathon bombing. There were a lot of different strategies in place to be able to get to the different layers of trauma and grief people [experience]. We are actively trying to train [our] staff to have the resources they need to be able to work with the population we work with. . . .

We all have to stay real, and available, and approachable. My father is ninety-nine and in amazing shape. He still does math in his head, and he can on paper. When I lose him, if I'm not real about it, then I'm not accessible. It's OK for educators to share their grief. It's OK for educators to share their anger about something that is wrong. It's OK for educators to share their excitement about things. The more our students feel our passions and our knowledge and our reasoning . . . I think there is cause and effect, and I think if we share all of our life experiences—the good, the bad, the sublime, and the ridiculous—that builds empathy and builds knowledge in our students. . . .

Tears are healing, and tears are healthy. My kids were raised on happy tears. Sometimes I cry when I'm happy more than I do when I'm sad. I cry when I'm moved. . . . I think emotions are a beautiful thing, and I think they give us strength. I know a lot of people have a hard time sharing their emotions. Mine are all over me.

I think because emotion comes naturally to me—it's probably good I went into theatre—people have an easier time opening up to me sometimes. [But] there's a certain point in production time when you've got to get your act together. . . . If you don't get your act together, you're going to make a fool of yourself and you're wasting my time; you're wasting your time. [I once had to tell some students] to get it together. . . . I shared my frustration. You have to be able to be a whole person.

Write and Reflect

Take two to five minutes to freewrite, without judgment, about a time when you felt compassion fatigue or burnout in a relationship. What about the other person led you to this point? What about your own positionality—your past experiences, present challenges, hopes, fears—contributed to your reaction? What helped you navigate this experience, and what might you change if you were to engage in this scenario again?

Next, list five to ten activities outside of work that you find regulatory. Refer to your drawing of a brain building from Chapter 1 for ideas. Next, list two to three people whom you feel comfortable speaking honestly with. Consider the individuals you included in your Connection Constellation from Chapter 4. To whom, and to what, can you turn?

Learning from Loss

Coda

Throughout this book, I've talked a lot about narratives—how the stories we live, the stories we tell ourselves, the stories we share, and the stories we receive shape how we perceive, process, and learn from loss. We have explored the ways in which grief changes our brains and behaviors and how culture, context, and secondary losses influence our subjective experiences of a universal inevitability. We learned about the ways in which structural inequities and ACE scores position certain students for resilience in the face of loss and force others to face a Gordian knot of roadblocks that require systemic change—not resilience—to surmount.

We also learned that supportive relationships are the most important protective guard against the ill effects of grief and early-life adversity. We learned that, although educators cannot and must not take on students' personal problems beyond their professional capacities, their presence, consistency, belief, and compassion all support students' self-regulation and make a profound difference in their lives.

Are these not, after all, the entities that we miss most when a loved one dies? Are they not the glue of human connection, the beauty of what it means to be here, together, in this moment? To connect and impact one another on this path?

I believe in the power of reciprocal vulnerability as much as I believe in the importance of appropriate boundaries. I believe that we have the power to change lives through small shifts in our approaches to student engagement. I take heart in the knowledge that we are not perfect; we're human, and that's all that grieving students need us to be.

You have the tools you need, now, to make a difference in the lives of your learners while protecting your own needs, too. As you consider how best to apply the practices explored in this book to your classroom, I urge you to return to the intentions you wrote in the introduction. Hold them close.

If ever you feel uncertain, bring them to mind and consider:

In a student's grief narrative, whom do you hope to be?

*A*s I wrote this book, it became apparent that every chapter could be a book and every subheading, a chapter—so nuanced is the new and necessary science surrounding developmental trauma and grief. I found the following resources and readings especially helpful, and I hope you do, too.

To access additional resources, as well as a complete grief responsive reading list, I invite you to visit my website www .GriefResponsiveTeaching.com, or Instagram @griefresponsive teaching, where I regularly share recommendations, materials, and learning opportunities.

The Science of Grief, Trauma, and Development

- *The Other Side of Sadness: What the New Science of Bereavement Tells Us About Life After Loss*, by George A. Bonanno

- *Before and After Loss: A Neurologist's Perspective on Loss, Grief, and Our Brain*, by Lisa M. Shulman

- *The Body Keeps the Score: Brain, Mind, and Body in the Healing of Trauma*, by Bessel van der Kolk

- *How Children Succeed: Grit, Curiosity, and the Hidden Power of Character*, by Paul Tough

- *Understanding Youth: Adolescent Development for Educators*, by Michael J. Nakkula and Eric Toshalis

- The Center for Youth Wellness (https://www .centerforyouthwellness.org/)

- The National Child Traumatic Stress Network (https://www .nctsn.org/)

- The Trauma Research Foundation (https://www
.traumaresearchfoundation.org/)

- Center on the Developing Child at Harvard University
(https://developingchild.harvard.edu/)

- National Association of School Psychologists (https://www
.nasponline.org/)

Grief-Responsive, Trauma-Informed Teaching and Student Support

- *Fostering Resilient Learners: Strategies for Creating a Trauma-Sensitive Classroom*, by Kristin Souers with Pete Hall

- *The Grieving Student: A Teacher's Guide*, by David J. Schonfeld and Marcia Quackenbush

- *Hope and Healing in Urban Education*, by Shawn Ginwright

- The National Center for School Crisis and Bereavement (https://www.schoolcrisiscenter.org/)

- The Coalition to Support Grieving Students (https://grievingstudents.org/)

- Dougy Center: The National Grief Center for Children and Families (https://www.dougy.org/)

- The National Alliance for Grieving Children (https://childrengrieve.org/)

Tools for Talking About Grief and End of Life

- *Let's Talk About Death (over Dinner): An Invitation and Guide to Life's Most Important Conversation*, by Michael Hebb

- *Being Mortal: Illness, Medicine and What Matters in the End*, by Atul Gawande

Mindfulness and Meditation

- Mindful Schools (https://www.mindfulschools.org/)
- Calm Schools Initiative (access the Calm app for free as a school!) (http://cdn.calm.com/documents/teachers-onboarding-manual.pdf)
- Mind Body Awareness Project (http://www.mbaproject.org/)

Self-Care for Teachers

- *The Courage to Teach: Exploring the Inner Landscape of a Teacher's Life*, by Parker J. Palmer
- The Center for Courage and Renewal (http://www.couragerenewal.org/)
- Option B (https://optionb.org/)
- Making Caring Common Project (https://mcc.gse.harvard.edu/)

References

Administration for Children and Families. n.d. "Secondary Traumatic Stress." US Department of Health and Human Services. Accessed September 13, 2020. https://www.acf.hhs.gov/trauma-toolkit/secondary-traumatic-stress.

Albom, Mitch. 2007. *Tuesdays with Morrie: An Old Man, a Young Man, and Life's Greatest Lesson.* New York: Crown.

Alschuler, Lise. 2019. "HPA Axis and Stress Response: Hypothalamic Pituitary Adrenal Axis." Integrative Therapeutics. Updated December 3. https://www .integrativepro.com/Resources/Integrative-Blog/2016/The-HPA-Axis.

American Federation of Teachers (AFT) and New York Life Foundation. 2012. "Grief in the Classroom: Groundbreaking Survey of Educators Shows Overwhelming Interest in Helping Grieving Students—and Strong Demand for Training, More Support." Press release. AFT and New York Life Foundation. December 10. https://www.aft.org/sites/default/files/release_bereavement121012.pdf.

———. 2020. "Educators Say COVID-19 Has Greatly Exacerbated the Grief Support Crisis in Schools, According to New Survey." Press release. AFT and New York Life Foundation. October 21. https://www.aft.org/press-release/educators-say -covid-19-has-greatly-exacerbated-grief-support-crisis-schools.

American Psychological Association. 2021. "Trauma." https://www.apa.org/topics /trauma.

Andrews, Evan. 2018. "What Was the Gordian Knot?" History (website). A and E Television Networks. August 29. https://www.history.com/news/what-was-the -gordian-knot.

Anwar, Yasmin. 2018. "Nature Is Proving to Be Awesome Medicine for PTSD." *Berkeley News*, July 12. https://news.berkeley.edu/2018/07/12/awe-nature-ptsd/.

Azab, Marwa. 2018. "Why Are Teens So Emotional?" *Psychology Today*, October 1. https://www.psychologytoday.com/us/blog/neuroscience-in-everyday-life /201810/why-are-teens-so-emotional.

Baicker, Karen. 2020. "The Impact of Secondary Trauma on Educators." *ASCD Express* 15 (13). http://www.ascd.org/ascd-express/vol15/num13/the-impact -of-secondary-trauma-on-educators.aspx.

Baikie, Karen A., and Kay Wilhelm. 2005. "Emotional and Physical Health Benefits of Expressive Writing." *Advances in Psychiatric Treatment* 11 (5): 338–46. doi:10.1192/apt.11.5.338.

Bath, Howard. 2008. "The Three Pillars of Trauma-Informed Care." *Reclaiming Children and Youth* 17 (3): 17–21. https://s3-us-west2.amazonaws.com/cxl/backup/prod /cxl/gklugiewicz/media/507188fa-30b7-8fd4-aa5f-ca6bb629a442.pdf.

Bhanoo, Sindya N. 2011. "How Meditation May Change the Brain." *Well* (blog). *The New York Times*, January 28. https://well.blogs.nytimes.com/2011/01/28 /how-meditation-may-change-the-brain/.

Bluestein, Jane. 2001. *Creating Emotionally Safe Schools: A Guide for Educators and Parents*. Deerfield Beach, FL: Health Communications.

Bonanno, George A. 2009. *The Other Side of Sadness: What the New Science of Bereavement Tells Us About Life After Loss*. New York: Basic Books.

Burke Harris, Nadine. 2018. *The Deepest Well: Healing the Long-Term Effects of Childhood Adversity*. Boston: Houghton Mifflin Harcourt.

Cain, Susan. 2015. "Why Your Life Story Matters and Why You Need to Tell It Now." *Psychology Today*, August 10. https://www.psychologytoday.com/us/blog /quiet-the-power-introverts/201508/why-your-life-story-matters-and-why-you -need-tell-it-now.

Center on the Developing Child. n.d. "Brain Architecture." Harvard University. Accessed September 7, 2020. https://developingchild.harvard.edu/science /key-concepts/brain-architecture/.

Centers for Disease Control and Prevention (CDC). 2020. "Behavioral Risk Factor Surveillance System ACE Data." US Department of Health and Human Services. Last reviewed April 3. https://www.cdc.gov/violenceprevention /childabuseandneglect/acestudy/ace-brfss.html.

Cheong, E Von, Carol Sinnott, Darren Dahly, and Patricia M Kearney. 2017. "Adverse Childhood Experiences (ACEs) and Later-Life Depression: Perceived Social Support as a Potential Protective Factor." *BMJ Open* 7 (9): 1–11. https:// bmjopen.bmj.com/content/bmjopen/7/9/e013228.full.pdf.

Chödrön, Pema. 1997. *When Things Fall Apart*. Boulder, CO: Shambhala.

Coalition to Support Grieving Students. n.d. "Grief Triggers." National Center for School Crisis and Bereavement. Accessed September 7, 2020. https:// grievingstudents.org/wp-content/uploads/2020/05/NYL-4D-GriefTriggers.pdf.

———. n.d. "What Not to Say." National Center for School Crisis and Bereavement. Accessed February 14, 2021. https://grievingstudents .org/wp-content/uploads/2020/05/NYL-1B-What-to-Say.pdf.

Coleman, Sheila. 2018. *Safe Kids Inc.: H.E.R.O. Curriculum: Grades K–8, Efficacy Findings in: Prominent Afterschool Program, Public School District, and Private School—Pilot Study Report*. Newport Beach, CA: Safe Kids. https:// safekidsinc.com/wp-content/uploads/2019/07 /Pilot-Study-Update.pdf.

Collaborative for Academic, Social and Emotional Learning (CASEL). 2021. "What Is SEL?" CASEL. https://casel.org/what-is-sel/.

Collins, Brittany R. 2019. "Responding to Students' Personal Narratives." Edutopia. George Lucas Education Foundation. February 7. https://www.edutopia.org /article/responding-students-personal-narratives.

Collins, Cory. 2019. "In Defense of Caring About Difference." *Teaching Tolerance*, September 5. https://www.tolerance.org/magazine/in-defense-of-caring -about-difference.

Congleton, Christina, Britta K. Hölzel, and Sara W. Lazar. 2015. "Mindfulness Can Literally Change Your Brain." *Harvard Business Review*, January 8. https://hbr .org/2015/01/mindfulness-can-literally-change-your-brain.

Counselling Central Admin. 2018. "The Egan Model and SOLER." Counselling Central. November 8. https://www.counsellingcentral.com/the-egan-model-and-soler/.

Cron, Lisa. 2012. *Wired for Story: The Writers Guide to Using Brain Science to Hook Readers from the Very First Sentence*. New York: Ten Speed.

Csikszentmihalyi, Mihaly. 2014. *Flow and the Foundations of Positive Psychology*. New York: Springer.

Daddona, Matthew. 2018. "The House That Marty Built: Lessons from a Legendary Poetry Teacher." *Teachers and Writers Magazine*, August 20. https://teachersandwritersmagazine.org/the-house-that-marty-built-lessons-from-a-legendary-poetry-teacher-5273.htm.

Devine, Megan. 2014. "You Aren't Here Now: How Grief and Mindfulness Don't Mix." *HuffPost*, April 13. https://www.huffpost.com/entry/grief-and-mindfulness_b_4757042.

Di Ciacco, Janis A. 2008. *The Colors of Grief: Understanding a Child's Journey Through Loss from Birth to Adulthood*. London: Jessica Kingsley.

Dillmann, Susanne M. 2010. "How Trauma Impacts Your Sense of Self: Part I." *GoodTherapy Blog*, May 6. https://www.goodtherapy.org/blog/identity-trauma/.

Doerr, Anthony. 2014. *All the Light We Cannot See*. New York: Scribner.

Dolan, Eric W. 2018. "Study Finds Evidence That 'Trigger Warnings' Can Be Psychologically Harmful." *PsyPost*, August 19. https://www.psypost.org/2018/08/study-finds-evidence-that-trigger-warnings-can-be-psychologically-harmful-52007.

Dweck, Carol. 2008. *Mindset: The New Psychology of Success*. New York: Ballantine Books.

EASEL Lab. n.d. "Navigate the Complex Field of Social and Emotional Learning." Explore SEL. Harvard Graduate School of Education. Accessed February 14, 2021. http://exploresel.gse.harvard.edu/.

Edutopia. 2011. "Social and Emotional Learning: A Short History." George Lucas Educational Foundation. October 6. https://www.edutopia.org/social-emotional-learning-history.

Ehmke, Rachel. n.d. "Helping Children Deal with Grief." Child Mind Institute. Accessed November 3, 2019. https://childmind.org/article/helping-children-deal-grief/.

Everytown Research and Policy. 2019. "The Impact of Gun Violence on Children and Teens." Everytown for Gun Safety Support Fund. May 29. https://everytownresearch.org/report/the-impact-of-gun-violence-on-children-and-teens/.

Facing History and Ourselves. 2021. "Text-to-Text, Text-to-Self, Text-to-World." Facing History and Ourselves. https://www.facinghistory.org/resource-library/teaching-strategies/text-text-text-self-text-world.

Ferlinghetti, Lawrence. 1958. *A Coney Island of the Mind: Poems*. New York: New Directions.

Fernández-Alcántara, Manuel, Miguel Pérez-García, M. N. Pérez-Marfil, Adrés Catena-Martínez, César Hueso-Montoro, and Francisco Cruz-Quintana. 2016. "Assessment of Different Components of Executive Function in Grief." *Psicothema* 28 (30): 260–65. https://www.ncbi.nlm.nih.gov/pubmed/27448258.

Flaherty, Colleen. 2018. "Dancing Backwards in High Heels: Study Finds Female Professors Experience More Work Demands and Special Favor Requests, Particularly from Academically Entitled Students." Inside Higher Ed. January 10. https://www.insidehighered.com/news/2018/01/10/study-finds-female-professors-experience-more-work-demands-and-special-favor.

Forman-Hoffman, Valerie L., Jonaki Bose, Kathryn R. Batts, Cristie Glasheen, Erica Hirsch, Rhonda S. Karg, Larke N. Huang, and Sarra L. Hedden. 2016. "Correlates of Lifetime Exposure to One or More Potentially Traumatic Events and Subsequent Posttraumatic Stress Among Adults in the United States: Results from the Mental Health Surveillance Study, 2008–2012." CBHSQ Data Review. Substance Abuse and Mental Health Services Administration. April. https://www.samhsa.gov/data/sites/default/files/CBHSQ-DR-PTSDtrauma-2016/CBHSQ-DR-PTSDtrauma-2016.htm.

Freire, Paulo. 1970. *Pedagogy of the Oppressed*. New York: Seabury.

Gaffney, Carrie. 2019. "When Schools Cause Trauma." *Teaching Tolerance* 62 (Summer). https://www.tolerance.org/magazine/summer-2019/when-schools-cause-trauma.

Gawande, Atul. 2010. *The Checklist Manifesto: How to Get Things Right*. New York: Henry Holt.

Ginwright, Shawn A. 2016. *Hope and Healing in Urban Education: How Urban Activists and Teachers Are Reclaiming Matters of the Heart*. New York: Routledge.

Gotink, Rinske A., Rozanna Meijboom, Meike W. Vernooij, Marion Smits, and M. G. Myriam Hunink. 2016. "8-Week Mindfulness Based Stress Reduction Induces Brain Changes Similar to Traditional Long-Term Meditation Practice—A Systematic Review." *Brain and Cognition* 108 (October): 32–41. https://www.ncbi.nlm.nih.gov/pubmed/27429096.

Gottschall, Jonathan. 2012. *The Storytelling Animal: How Stories Make Us Human*. Boston: Houghton Mifflin.

Greater Good Science Center at the University of California, Berkeley. 2021. "Mindfulness Defined." *Greater Good Magazine*. https://greatergood.berkeley.edu/topic/mindfulness/definition.

Guidi, Jenny, Marcella Lucente, Nicoletta Sonino, and Giovanni A. Fava. 2020. "Allostatic Load and Its Impact on Health: A Systematic Review." *Psychotherapy and Psychosomatics* 90 (1): 1–17. https://www.karger.com/Article/FullText/510696.

Guy-Evans, Olivia. 2020. "Bronfenbrenner's Ecological Systems Theory." *Simply Psychology*, November 9. https://www.simplypsychology.org/Bronfenbrenner.html.

Haley, Eleanor. 2015. "Understanding Avoidance in Grief." *What's Your Grief?* (blog), February 17. https://whatsyourgrief.com/avoidance-in-grief/.

Hammond, Zaretta. 2014. *Culturally Responsive Teaching and the Brain: Promoting Authentic Engagement and Rigor Among Culturally and Linguistically Diverse Students*. Thousand Oaks, CA: Corwin.

Harris, Darcy L., and Howard R. Winokuer. 2019. *Principles and Practices of Grief Counseling*. 3rd ed. New York: Springer. https://connect.springerpub.com/content/book/978-0-8261-7333-1.

Harvard Health Publishing. 2011. "Understanding the Stress Response." The President and Fellows of Harvard College. March. https://www.health.harvard.edu/staying-healthy/understanding-the-stress-response.

Haven, Kendall. 2007. *Story Proof: The Science Behind the Startling Power of Story*. Westport, CT: Libraries Unlimited.

Hawkins Centers of Learning. n.d. "I, Thou, and It." Hawkins Centers of Learning. Accessed September 12, 2020. http://www.hawkinscenters.org/i-thou-and-it.html.

Hawkins, David. 2002. *The Informed Vision: Essays on Learning and Human Nature*. New York: Algora.

Hebb, Michael. 2018. *Let's Talk About Death (over Dinner)*. New York: De Capo.

Hemingway, Ernest. 2017. "A Clean, Well-Lighted Place." In *The Short Stories of Ernest Hemingway: The Hemingway Library Edition*. New York: Scribner.

Herrmann, Ned. 1997. "What Is the Function of the Various Brainwaves?" *Scientific American*, December 22. https://www.scientificamerican.com/article/what-is-the-function-of-t-1997-12-22/.

History.com editors. 2009. "Columbine Shooting." History. A and E Television Networks. November 9. https://www.history.com/topics/1990s/columbine-high-school-shootings.

hooks, bell. 2003. *Teaching Community*. Abingdon, UK: Psychology Press.

Hunt, Elle. 2019. "Blue Spaces: Why Time Spent Near Water Is the Secret of Happiness." *The Guardian*, November 3. https://www.theguardian.com/lifeandstyle/2019/nov/03/blue-space-living-near-water-good-secret-of-happiness.

Institute on Trauma and Trauma-Informed Care. 2016. "Interview on Grief and Loss with Roger, a Survivor." Transcript. *Trauma Talks* (podcast). University at Buffalo. January 15. http://socialwork.buffalo.edu/content/dam/socialwork/social-research/ITTIC/Trauma Talks Transcripts/Roger.pdf.

Intrator, Sam M., and Megan Scribner. 2003. *Teaching with Fire: Poetry That Sustains the Courage to Teach*. San Francisco: Jossey-Bass.

Jacobs, Douglas. n.d. "Emotional Differences Response Chart." Mental Health America of Eastern Missouri. Accessed February 14, 2021. https://mha-em.org/im-looking-for/mental-health-knowledge-base/concerns/56-emotional-differences-response-chart.

Jung, Carl G. 1981. *The Development of Personality: Papers on Child Psychology, Education, and Related Subjects*. Translated by R. F. C. Hull. Princeton, NJ: Princeton University Press.

Kakar, Vani, and Nanki Oberoi. 2016. "Mourning with Social Media: Rewiring Grief." *Indian Journal of Positive Psychology* 7 (3). 371–75. http://www.academia.edu/28899909/Mourning_with_Social_Media_Rewiring_Grief?email_work_card=title.

Kübler-Ross, Elisabeth. (1969) 2014. *On Death and Dying: What the Dying Have to Teach Doctors, Nurses, Clergy and Their Own Families.* With a Foreword by Ira Byock. New York: Scribner.

Lamott, Anne. n.d. "An Homage to Age and Femininity." *O Magazine.* Reprinted on *Flourish Flash Blog*, August 11, 2009. https://flourishpdx.wordpress.com/2009 /08/11/an-homage-to-age-and-femininity/.

Lander, Jessica. 2018. "Helping Teachers Manage the Weight of Trauma." *Usable Knowledge*, September 26. https://www.gse.harvard.edu/news/uk/18/09/helping -teachers-manage-weight-trauma.

Larson, Jennifer. 2019. "What Are Alpha Brain Waves and Why Are They Important?" Healthline. October 9. https://www.healthline.com/health/alpha-brain-waves.

Lawrence-Lightfoot, Sara. 2000. *Respect: An Exploration.* New York: Basic Books.

L'Engle, Madeleine. 2016. *Walking on Water: Reflections on Faith and Art.* New York: Convergent Books.

Lorde, Audre. 2017. *Burst of Light: And Other Essays.* Garden City, NY: Ixia.

Low, Phillip. 2020. "Overview of the Autonomic Nervous System—Brain, Spinal Cord, and Nerve Disorders." *Merck Manual Consumer Version.* Merck. April. https:// www.merckmanuals.com/home/brain,-spinal-cord,-and-nerve-disorders /autonomic-nervous-system-disorders/overview-of-the-autonomic -nervous-system.

Lunkenheimer, Erika, Alex Busuito, Kayla M. Brown, Carlomagno Panlilio, and Elizabeth A. Skowron. 2019. "The Interpersonal Neurobiology of Child Maltreatment: Parasympathetic Substrates of Interactive Repair in Maltreating and Nonmaltreating Mother–Child Dyads." *Child Maltreatment* 24 (4): 353–63. doi:10.1177/1077559518824058.

Mackesy, Charlie. 2019. *The Boy, the Mole, the Fox and the Horse.* New York: HarperOne.

Magliano, Joseph. 2015. "Why Are Teen Brains Designed for Risk-Taking?" *Psychology Today*, June 9. https://www.psychologytoday.com/us/blog/the-wide-wide -world-psychology/201506/why-are-teen-brains-designed-risk-taking.

McLeod, Saul. 2020. "Maslow's Hierarchy of Needs." *Simply Psychology*, December 29. https://www.simplypsychology.org/maslow.html.

McOwen, Alex. 2020. "Lifelines: How COVID-19 Creates 'Pre-Traumatic Conditions' in the Brain." Interviewed by Peter Biello. NHPR. May 4. https://www.nhpr.org /post/lifelines-how-covid-19-creates-pre-traumatic-conditions-brain.

McRaven, William H. 2017. *Make Your Bed: Little Things That Can Change Your Life . . . and Maybe the World.* Waterville, ME: Thorndike.

Miller, Ashley. 2019. "How to Boost Your Alpha Brain Waves (And Why You Should Care." Healthfully. June 13. https://healthfully.com/how-to-boost-your -alpha-brain-waves-and-why-you-should-care-7447143.html.

Mindful Schools. 2019. "About Us." Mindful Schools. https://www.mindfulschools.org /about/.

Nadworny, Elissa. 2015. "Grief in the Classroom: 'Saying Nothing Says a Lot.'" NPR Ed. January 13. https://www.npr.org/sections/ed/2015/01/13/376720559 /grieving-in-the-classroom.

Nakkula, Michael J., and Eric Toshalis. 2006. *Understanding Youth: Adolescent Development for Educators.* Cambridge, MA: Harvard Education Press.

NASP School Safety and Crisis Response Committee. 2015. "Addressing Grief: Tips for Teachers and Administrators." Bethesda, MD: National Association of School Psychologists. https://www.nasponline.org/resources-and-publications /resources-and-podcasts/school-climate-safety-and-crisis/mental-health -resources/addressing-grief/addressing-grief-tips-for-teachers-and -administrators.

National Child Traumatic Stress Network (NCTSN), Secondary Traumatic Stress Committee. 2011. *Secondary Traumatic Stress: A Fact Sheet for Child-Serving Professionals.* Los Angeles and Durham, NC: National Center for Child Traumatic Stress. https://www.nctsn.org/sites/default/files/resources/fact-sheet /secondary_traumatic_stress_child_serving_professionals.pdf.

NBC News. 2018. "How Grief Affects Your Brain and What to Do About It." Better by Today, September 11. Video, 3:05. https://www.nbcnews.com/better/video /how-grief-affects-your-brain-and-what-to-do-about-it-1255640131592.

Niemiec, Christopher P., and Richard M. Ryan. 2009. "Autonomy, Competence, and Relatedness in the Classroom: Applying Self-Determination Theory to Educational Practice." *Theory and Research in Education* 7 (2): 133–44. doi:10.1177/1477878509104318.

Nye, Naomi Shihab. 1995. *Words Under the Words: Selected Poems.* Portland, OR: Eighth Mountain.

Oppland, Mike. 2021. "8 Ways to Create Flow According to Mihaly Csikszentmihalyi." *PositivePsychology* (blog), February 15. https://positivepsychology.com /mihaly-csikszentmihalyi-father-of-flow/.

Pai, Anushka, Alina M. Suris, and Carol S. North. 2017. "Posttraumatic Stress Disorder in the DSM-5: Controversy, Change, and Conceptual Considerations." *Behavioral Sciences* 7 (1): 7. doi: 10.3390/bs7010007.

Palmer, Parker J. 2000. *Let Your Life Speak: Listening for the Voice of Vocation.* San Francisco: Jossey-Bass.

———. 2010. *The Courage to Teach: Exploring the Inner Landscape of a Teacher's Life.* Hoboken, NJ: John Wiley.

Paterson, Katherine. 1979. *Bridge to Terabithia.* New York: Avon.

Patton, Desmond Upton, Jamie Macbeth, Sarita Schoenebeck, Katherine Shear, and Kathleen McKeown. 2018. "Accommodating Grief on Twitter: An Analysis of Expressions of Grief Among Gang Involved Youth on Twitter Using Qualitative Analysis and Natural Language Processing." *Biomedical Informatics Insights* 10: 1–9. https://journals.sagepub.com/doi/full/10.1177/1178222618763155.

Pennebaker, James W. 2017. "Expressive Writing in Psychological Science." *Perspectives on Psychological Science* 13 (2): 226–29. doi:10.1177/1745691617707315.

Pierson, Rita. 2013. "Every Kid Needs a Champion." Filmed in April at TED Talks Education, New York, NY. TED video, 7:24. https://www.ted.com/talks /rita_pierson_every_kid_needs_a_champion?language=en.

Porges, Stephen W. 2009. "The Polyvagal Theory: New Insights into Adaptive Reactions of the Autonomic Nervous System." *Cleveland Clinic Journal of Medicine* 76 (suppl. 2): S86–90. doi:10.3949/ccjm.76.s2.17.

Pressley, Jana. 2020. "The Complexity of Adaptation to Trauma." (Accessible upon paying for trauma certification.) Lecture, PESI and the Trauma Research Foundation's Certificate in Traumatic Stress Studies. PESI. https://catalog .pesi.com/Classroom/ClassroomProductsDescription?classroomI=945.

Pynoos, Robert S., Alan M. Steinberg, Christopher M. Layne, Li-Jung Liang, Rebecca L. Vivrette, Ernestine C. Briggs, Cassandra Kisiel, Mandy Habib, Thomas R. Belin, and John A. Fairbank. 2014. "Modeling Constellations of Trauma Exposure in the National Child Traumatic Stress Network Core Data Set." *Psychological Trauma: Theory, Research, Practice, and Policy* 6 (suppl. 1): S9–S17. doi:10.1037/a0037767.

Reilly, Katie. 2018. "The Location of the Florida High School Shooting Was Recently Named the Safest City in the State." *Time*, February 15. https://time.com /5159277/parkland-florida-high-school-shooting-safest-city/.

Rogers, Fred. 1977. Lifetime Achievement award acceptance speech. Presented at the 24th Daytime Emmy Awards, New York, NY, May 21.

Ruedo, M. Rosario, and Pedro M. Paz-Alonso. 2013. "Executive Functions: Executive Function and Emotional Development." In *Encyclopedia on Early Childhood Development* (online), edited by Richard E. Tremblay, Michel Boivin, and Ray DeV. Peters. http://www.child-encyclopedia.com/executive-functions /according-experts/executive-function-and-emotional-development.

Sacks, Oliver. 2019. "Oliver Sacks: The Healing Power of Gardens." *The New York Times*, April 18. https://www.nytimes.com/2019/04/18/opinion/sunday/oliver -sacks-gardens.html.

Schonfeld, David J. 1993. "Talking with Children About Death." *Journal of Pediatric Health Care* 7 (6): 269–74. doi:10.1016/s0891-5245(06)80008-8.

Schonfeld, David J., and Marcia Quackenbush. 2009. *After a Loved One Dies—How Children Grieve*. New York: New York Life Foundation. https://www.aap.org /en-us/advocacy-and-policy/aap-health-initiatives/Children-and-Disasters /Documents/After-a-Loved-One-Dies-English.pdf.

Schulte, Brigid. 2015. "Harvard Neuroscientist: Meditation Not Only Reduces Stress, Here's How It Changes Your Brain." *The Washington Post*, May 26. https:// www.washingtonpost.com/news/inspired-life/wp/2015/05/26/harvard -neuroscientist-meditation-not-only-reduces-stress-it-literally-changes -your-brain/.

Schwartz, Katrina. 2019. "Why Mindfulness and Trauma-Informed Teaching Don't Always Go Together." *MindShift*, January 27. https://www.kqed.org /mindshift/52881/why-mindfulness-and-trauma-informed-teaching-dont -always-go-together.

Shafer, Gregory. 2017. "Dealing with and Writing About Death." *English Journal* 107 (2): 35–40. https://library.ncte.org/journals/EJ/issues/v107-2/29353.

Shafer, Leah. 2018. "The Experiences of Teachers of Color." *Usable Knowledge*, June 12. https://www.gse.harvard.edu/news/uk/18/06/experiences-teachers-color.

Shakespeare, William. (1599) 1992. *Hamlet (Folger Shakespeare Library)*. Edited by Barbara A. Mowat and Paul Werstine. New York: Simon and Schuster.

Shear, M. Katherine. 2012. "Grief and Mourning Gone Awry: Pathway and Course of Complicated Grief." *Dialogues in Clinical Neuroscience* 14 (2): 119–28. https://www.ncbi.nlm.nih.gov/pmc/articles/PMC3384440/.

Shulman, Lisa M. 2018. *Before and After Loss: A Neurologist's Perspective on Loss, Grief, and Our Brain*. Baltimore: Johns Hopkins University Press.

Slaninova, Gabriela, and Martina Stainerova. 2015. "Trauma as a Component of the Self-Concept of Undergraduates." *Procedia—Social and Behavioral Sciences* 171: 465–71. doi:10.1016/j.sbspro.2015.01.148.

Souers, Kristin, and Peter A. Hall. 2016. *Fostering Resilient Learners: Strategies for Creating a Trauma-Sensitive Classroom*. Alexandria, VA: ASCD.

Spinks, Sarah. 2002. "Introduction to Inside the Teenage Brain." *Frontline*. January 31. WGBH Boston. https://www.pbs.org/wgbh/pages/frontline/shows/teenbrain/etc/synopsis.html.

Sprague, Nadav, David Berrigan, and Christine C. Ekenga. 2020. "An Analysis of the Educational and Health-Related Benefits of Nature-Based Environmental Education in Low-Income Black and Hispanic Children." *Health Equity* 4 (1): 198–210. doi:10.1089/heq.2019.0118.

Springfield Public Schools. 2017. "Springfield Central High School 2017–018 School Profile." Central High School. https://central.springfieldpublicschools.com/UserFiles/Servers/Server_499768/File/Central High School-School Profile.pdf.

Starecheski, Laura. 2015. "Take The ACE Quiz—and Learn What It Does and Doesn't Mean." Shots. NPR. March 2. https://www.npr.org/sections/health-shots/2015/03/02/387007941/take-the-ace-quiz-and-learn-what-it-does-and-doesnt-mean.

Steele, Claude. 2011. *Whistling Vivaldi: How Stereotypes Affect Us and What We Can Do*. New York: W. W. Norton.

Style, Emily. 1988. "Curriculum As Window and Mirror." *Listening for All Voices*. Summit, NJ: Oak Knoll School monograph. https://nationalseedproject.org/Key-SEED-Texts/curriculum-as-window-and-mirror.

Substance Abuse and Mental Health Services Administration. 2019. "Trauma and Violence." US Department of Health and Human Services. August 2. https://www.samhsa.gov/trauma-violence.

Suttie, Jill. 2016. "How to Listen to Pain." *Greater Good Magazine*, February 17. https://greatergood.berkeley.edu/article/item/how_to_listen_to_pain.

Thelen, Veronica. 2007. "Disenfranchised Grief." *Mental Health Matters* 4 (10). https://www.thpcc.com/disenfranchised-grief.

Thomas, Angie. 2017. *The Hate U Give*. New York: Balzer and Bray/Harperteen.

Tough, Paul. 2012. *How Children Succeed: Grit, Curiosity, and the Hidden Power of Character*. Reprint, New York: Mariner Books.

Towles, Amor. 2016. *A Gentleman in Moscow*. New York: Penguin Books.

University of Massachusetts Medical School. 2014. "Jon Kabat-Zinn." (Page deleted.) UMass Medical School. June 24. https://www.umassmed.edu/cfm/about-us /people/2-meet-our-faculty/kabat-zinn-profile/.

Urist, Jacoba. 2016. "The Art and Science of Apologizing." *The Atlantic*, February 23. https://www.theatlantic.com/science/archive/2016/02/how-to-apologize/470457/.

van der Kolk, Bessel. 2000. "Posttraumatic Stress Disorder and the Nature of Trauma." *Dialogues in Clinical Neuroscience* 2 (1): 7–22.

———. 2014. *The Body Keeps the Score: Brain, Mind, and Body in the Healing of Trauma*. New York: Penguin Books.

Wagner, Dee. 2016. "Polyvagal Theory in Practice." *Counseling Today*, June 27. https:// ct.counseling.org/2016/06/polyvagal-theory-practice/.

Walton, Alice G. 2015. "7 Ways Meditation Can Actually Change the Brain." *Forbes*, February 9. https://www.forbes.com/sites/alicegwalton/2015/02/09/7-ways -meditation-can-actually-change-the-brain/#a4c1c9914658.

Whitman, Walt. 1891. "O Me! O Life!" Poets.org. Academy of American Poets. https:// poets.org/poem/o-me-o-life.

Williams, Litsa. 2013. "Secondary Loss—One Loss Isn't Enough??!!" *What's Your Grief?* (blog), July 22. https://whatsyourgrief.com/secondary-loss-one-loss-isnt -enough/.

Winfrey, Oprah. 2018. "Treating Childhood Trauma." Transcript of *60 Minutes* segment. CBS News. CBS Interactive. March 11. https://www.cbsnews.com/news/oprah -winfrey-treating-childhood-trauma.

Zak, Paul J. 2012. *The Moral Molecule: The Source of Love and Prosperity*. New York: Dutton.